Accounting Fraud

Accounting Fraud

Maneuvering and Manipulation, Past and Present

Gary Giroux

First published in 2014 by
Business Expert Press, LLC
222 East 46th Street, New York, NY 10017
www.businessexpertpress.com

ISBN-13: 978-1-60649-628-2 (paperback)
ISBN-13: 978-1-60649-629-9 (e-book)

Business Expert Press Financial Accounting and Auditing Collection

Collection ISSN: 2151-2795 (print)
Collection ISSN: 2151-2817 (electronic)

Cover and interior design by Exeter Premedia Services Private Ltd., Chennai, India

First edition: 2014

10 9 8 7 6 5 4 3 2 1

Printed in the United States of America.

Abstract

Scandals relating to manipulation and fraud have dominated much of the history of business and the accounting profession in America since its founding. Crooks, corruption, scandals, and panics have been regular features of the business landscape ever since, with regulations and the expansion of financial disclosure, auditing, and regulatory agencies following major debacles. Prior to the creation of the Securities and Exchange Commission (SEC) in the 1930s and the development of generally accepted accounting principles (GAAP), few accounting rules existed and it is difficult to identify "accounting" scandals. Consequently, the primary focus is the post–World War II period, when accounting manipulation and fraud can be identified based on specific accounting violations.

The importance of this topic is demonstrated by the major accounting and finance scandals of the 21st century, some of the most destructive in our history. Enron may be the most extensive manipulation and fraud case in terms of multiple accounting-related abuses over an extended period of time. The multitrillion dollar real estate crises is the most gigantic and widespread and, seemingly, could have been easily avoided (it took a number of "fail-safe" failures for the financial system to crash). This pair of scandals has an extensive number of companions (if less severe and not as well known). The types of violations, causes, and results are equally valid today—these and similar issues continue to be of major concern.

Key points include the importance of incentive structures of key players and the need for effective regulation, which become more obvious by considering multi-decades of abuse. Executive compensation, pensions, special purpose entities, and derivatives continue to be accounting issues as they have for decades.

This short book can be used as a supplementary source in introductory financial accounting courses (elementary and intermediate), accounting- and finance-related MBA courses, and business history. The book can also be used as part of forensic accounting and fraud detection for continuing education. In addition, it can be useful for accounting and finance professionals wanting exposure to financial disclosure issues and other accounting risks, plus executives looking to expand their knowledge of accounting fraud and risk areas.

Keywords

accounting fraud, accounting standards, auditors, big 4 accounting firms, corporate fraud, earnings manipulation, earnings quality, Enron, Sarbanes-Oxley act, securities and exchange commission, subprime meltdown, transparency, WorldCom

Contents

Introduction

Accounting fraud does tend to come in waves, and is discovered most often after a market collapse, since no one is interested in investigating much when stock prices are high and everyone's making big money.
—Barbara Toffler

The purpose of accounting is providing information and control. Audited financial statements provide assurance that the financial and other information is accurate and fully disclosed based on existing rules. However, key providers of that information may be unwilling to present accurate and complete disclosure. The incentives to cheat can be substantial and those at the top may be especially ethically-challenged and greedy.

Business history includes incredible examples of disgraceful acts and, to some extent, scandal becomes a central part of the story of economic history. To get certain things done, corruption could be encouraged—political machines in major cities or states, for example, could become amazingly efficient ensuring businesses quickly accommodated after appropriate "consulting fees." The second half of the 19th century was almost certainly the most corrupt in American history, but also one of the greatest periods of economic growth and innovation. Successful entrepreneurs and managers had little choice but deal with the dark side—many, of course, did it with gusto.

George Washington assumed the presidency in 1789, but before the end of his term in office, the country has a revolt (the Whiskey Rebellion), a financial scandal (the Panic of 1792), and the first real estate scam (Georgia's Yazoo land scandal). Along with the founding fathers was a list of founding villains (usually successful men with a dark side), including speculator, politician and thief William Blount; incompetent general and spy James Wilkinson; plus financial manipulator, political deal maker, and future vice president Aaron Burr, later indicted for treason.

Government regulation to combat corruption started early, including law codes from antiquity such as the Code of Hammurabi (1772 BC).

Government action was not particularly effective; even the threat of beheading did not put a dent in corruption. As economies got larger and more complex, legislation and enforcement expanded, sometimes effective, sometimes not so much. The American constitution of 1788 established federal responsibilities and left the regulations of corporations primarily up to the states—but Washington maintained the responsibility over interstate commerce. The United States was a more-or-less laissez faire economy similar to the description by economist Adam Smith in *The Wealth of Nations*, with little interference from government. Problems grew as businesses expanded and owners desired both monopoly power and great wealth. Corporate growth brought expansion across states lines, resulting in the inability of states to deal with rising commerce. Political history includes the dynamic patchwork of state and federal experiments with regulations. Business, in the meantime, sought regulatory responses for its own benefit—with little if any concern for the public interest.

Stories of American exceptionalism abound in the first century of industrial growth. From an agricultural backwater the U.S. became the industrial giant of the world by the end of the 19th century. Brilliant inventors from Eli Whitney and Samuel Morse to Alexander Graham Bell and Thomas Edison transfixed the lives of most Americans—as did entrepreneurs from Cornelius Vanderbilt to John D. Rockefeller and Andrew Carnegie. Speculators from Daniel Drew to Jay Gould proved equally innovative if less productive to broad economic interests—they were called Robber Barons for a reason. Success in both camps typically required ruthless behavior and it could be difficult to tell the heroes from the crooks—Vanderbilt, Rockefeller, and Carnegie were on most 19th century Robber Baron lists.

Accounting was a necessary part of the economic landscape. Early business relied on techniques similar to Italian merchants of the late Middle Ages. As businesses got big, especially railroads, the need for information required new accounting methods to understand and control costs and set prices, the requirements for cash and financing, and providing the necessary information to attract investors. Railroad managers in the mid-19th century developed many of these new techniques. Just as some railroad executives were forward thinkers, others were interested in manipulation and obfuscation to promote their own schemes. Jay Gould, for example, in control of several railroads at various times was predominately a speculator and made as much money driving down the price of his companies as driving them up—with little regard for actual corporate profitability or the long-term needs of his railroads. Although corrupt, his techniques were legal at the time (or at least never prosecuted). In fact, only a few of the 19th century villains were convicted and sentenced to jail, such as Boss Tweed of New York City's Tammany Hall (the Democratic political machine). His crimes involved multiple examples of outright fraud, with bribery (a payment to influence conduct) and extortion (obtaining a payment through coercion) particular favorites.

After the corrupt Gilded Age (named by Mark Twain for the period of the recovery from the Panic of 1873 to the Panic of 1893), progressives gained power and attempts at real reform followed. The Interstate Commerce Commission, formed in 1887 to regulate railroads, became the first federal agency to restrain illicit business practices. The Sherman Antitrust Act followed in 1890 with modest success limiting business conspiracies and monopoly power. State regulations were a mixed bag. State banking regulations could be conservative and serve the public interest or allow wildcat banking with little oversight at all. Some states attempted to limit business monopoly powers, ban unsafe and unsanitary practices, or offer some protections for labor. Other states became servile to business. New Jersey offered the most liberal incorporation laws, allowing big corporations to create holding companies controlling operations across the country. The development of concentration and monopoly power in dozens of industries was possible because of the New Jersey laws.

The 1920s was an anything-goes financial period, with investor euphoria, a stock market bubble, and corruption in multiple forms. The 1929 market crash helped bring on a Great Depression. The Congressional Pecora Hearings uncovered substantial corruption but few illegal acts (mainly income tax violations), but still shocking the public. The result was the New Deal of President Franklin Roosevelt and the creation of the Securities and Exchange Commission (SEC) and other financial reforms. Wall Street was restructured and the regulatory process started the creation of a formal accounting system (soon to be called generally accepted accounting standards or GAAP) and standardized financial audits.

After World War II America was the global economic colossus, producing half the world's output with the most productive manufacturing processes anywhere. Accounting, particularly managerial accounting, also was highly sophisticated and advanced, with computers just being introduced. Formal accounting and financial reporting procedures were developing nicely and the SEC maintained considerable control over and respect of financial markets. For the next thirty or so years (depending on what measures to focus on), the country maintained global economic and financial leadership. Corruption and fraud generally were small scale, either big frauds at small companies such as ZZZZ Best or small (and often obscure) frauds as major corporations such as General Electric.

Inflation, intense foreign competition with improved manufacturing methods, and finally "stagflation" (the simultaneous rise of both inflation and economic stagnation) brought severe economic and financial problems. Financial "innovations," often involving accounting issues (such as acquisition accounting techniques), led to increasingly illicit acts (hostile takeovers, junk bonds, and insider trading to name a few) resulting in financial markets and corporate headquarters becoming nastier places. The "Reagan Revolution" (or more accurately the tough love of Federal Reserve Chairman Paul Volcker) tamed inflation in the early 1980s and the economy and stock market boomed. The computer and Internet revolutions of the 1990s led to the tech bubble, ridiculous stock prices, and corporations behaving badly. After the tech collapse in the new millennium, the world discovered the horrendous corruption of major corporations including Enron and WorldCom. One result was the Sarbanes-Oxley Act of 2002, a major regulatory overhaul.

The major economic story of the 21st century was the rapid growth of the banking and financial world, concentrated on the financial manipulations of structured finance, compounded by illicit use (and little regulation) of derivatives (contracts derived from existing contracts such as forwards and options) and special purpose entities (legal entities created for specific purposes). These techniques (reasonable financial innovations in and of themselves) were used in such an outrageous fashion that the resulting subprime meltdown almost destroyed the financial world.

Instead, the Federal Reserve (America's central bank, responsible for monetary policy though money supply and interest rates) and Treasury Department (executive department to manage revenue and debt) invested in a multi-trillion dollar bailout of the banking system. Despite all the regulations on the books, financial and accounting manipulations were worse than ever (at least in total dollar terms)—corresponding to the misaligned incentives of the key players, especially the outrageous compensation of banking executives.

This is the story I want to tell in this book: defining the various illicit financial and accounting acts over time (with considerable overlap over the last 200 plus years), attempting to identify the major perpetrators and the reasons for their actions, determining what regulations were effective and why, and using the historical evidence to attempt to predict the future. No question, there will be more manipulation and fraud. The historical evidence, reinforced by psychology and economics, points to the critical importance of the incentives of key players whatever the existing institutional framework. Describing incentives in place and how they can go awry is a critical part of the historical analysis and predicting future abuse.

Accounting fraud and manipulation are summarized in seven chapters. The first chapter introduces the dynamic environment of deceit and illicit acts, and why the major players (even if rich and successful) would be willing to commit heinous acts. The roles of regulation and disclosure are explored, including when and why they are either successful or failures (or some combination of the two). The next five chapters cover American business, scandals and attempts at reform, in roughly chronological order. Chapter Two covers the broad period before the reforms of the New Deal. Chapter Three looks at the Great Depression in some detail. The Securities and Exchange Commission, other federal regulations and private sector reforms (such as establishing accounting standards) are still of considerable importance today. Chapter Four covers the post-World War II period through the savings and loan crisis of the 1980s, with a focus on the movement from relative honesty in industrial and financial markets to the development of pockets of extreme corruption—perhaps the start of modern accounting and auditing issues. Chapter Five reviews the 1990s and early 21st century, including the rise and collapse of the tech bubble. Particular attention is paid to Enron, perhaps the greatest corporate fraud case in American history. In terms of perverse incentives, corruption through government and financial markets, massive use of deceit and reporting of bogus numbers, and violating regulatory and disclosure requirement at every level, Enron had it all. Chapter Six covers the strange story of the subprime meltdown, creating a financial crisis of epic proportions—out of the safest of credit instruments, the mortgage (accounting was a bit player here). Chapter Seven sums up historical finding and considers key points for predicting future abuse. The major frustration of speculating about the future is the continued existence of perverse incentives within financial markets, politics, and global corporations.

CHAPTER 1

Accounting Scandals, a Historical Perspective

Is it possible that scandal is somehow an essential ingredient in capitalism? That a healthy free-market economy must tempt a certain number of people to behave corruptly, and that a certain number of these will do so? That the crooks are not a sign that something is rotten but that something is working more or less as it was meant to work?

—Michael Lewis

The Role of Accounting, Financial Disclosure, and Auditing

Accounting, defined broadly, includes all aspects of keeping track of monetary and other business transactions for individuals, corporations, and other institutions. These records are used internally for management control and decisions. Periodic financial statements are issued to provide information to investors and other interested outsiders. Accounting started with the use of barter by merchant traders before the dawn of history, with archaeological findings suggesting the starting point of record keeping in the Fertile Crescent some 10,000 years ago. Italian merchants in the late Middle Ages developed double entry bookkeeping. Accounting sophistication increased as business expanded and economic complexity increased. Those mastering double entry had a competitive advantage and became more likely to succeed.

Northern Europe innovations included the joint stock company, stock exchanges, and the many inventions leading to the Industrial Revolution and factory production. Factory owners typically made little use of accounting until forced by desperation to figure out costs and how they made money, usually during depressions when sales collapsed. The vast majority of the firms did not adjust and failed. Eighteenth-century British Potter Josiah Wedgwood was one who used accounting to avoid bankruptcy during the depression of 1772 and build an increasingly thriving business. He had to understand cost accounting in enough detail to know the costs of specific products, where to save money, and how to adjust prices. Wedgwood improved the record keeping in enough detail to determine expenses for materials and labor for each manufacturing step for each product. For the first time, he discovered specifically what each product cost and adjusted sales prices accordingly. Wedgwood figured out that his high fixed costs encouraged increasing volume. His markets were roughly divided between high-price high-quality products for richer customers and lower-cost lower-price products for the rest. Focusing only on the needs of the wealthy, although lucrative, did not produce enough sales to make money, given the high fixed costs.

In the United States, accounting was initially primitive (not much different from Italian counterparts of the late Middle Ages) and improved as the need arose for better information, for roughly the same reasons as Wedgwood. Progress was made in New England textile manufacturing as it became larger, integrated, and more complex. Considerable progress was made by railroads especially in cost and managerial accounting as professional managers needed considerable timely information on railroad operations that became increasingly complex and costly. Andrew Carnegie adapted many of the accounting methods developed at the Pennsylvania Railroad (where he received his initial training) to make his steel empire the most efficient and lowest-cost producer in the country. Other manufacturing companies were making similar progress. By early in the 20th century, Du Pont developed the most advanced cost accounting system around, including the use of return on investment (ROI) and the Du Pont model for decomposing income.

Industrial accounting reached its mid-20th-century zenith at General Motors (GM) under President Alfred Sloan and controller Donaldson Brown. The accounting system of Du Pont was adopted and expanded (Du Pont acquired a controlling interest in GM before 1920). GM became the biggest manufacturing firm in the world by the mid-20th century, with arguably the most efficient manufacturing system in a decentralized structure. This structure worked because of the detailed accounting records maintained at the factory floor level and quickly delivered and analyzed by the centralized staff. By the 1960s, a host of problems including the rise of efficient Japanese and other foreign manufacturers began a relative decline at GM and other American manufacturers. Japanese systems focused on quality and various forms of efficiency eventually revolutionized manufacturing literally around the world. The rise of computers, the Internet, and robots and other forms of automation again changed the nature of manufacturing accounting.

Financial Disclosure

Financial statement and other disclosures typically presented in an annual report summarize the financial position, earnings, and cash flows to allow outsiders to have a reasonable financial understanding of the underlying business for the fiscal year. While most companies viewed financial information as proprietary and refused to release information unless absolutely necessary (such as to get a bank loan), balance sheets and other financial disclosure became more common in the 19th century as railroads and other large businesses issued financial reports to attract investors into their stocks and bonds in the capital markets.

Throughout the 19th century, stock and bond investors relied on cash dividend and interest payments rather than earnings (an income statement was viewed with skepticism before formal accounting standards were developed in the mid-20th century). Standardized financial disclosures evolved as the Securities and Exchange Commission (SEC) and the private sector bodies issued accounting standards (the Committee on Accounting Procedure, Accounting Principles Board, and the Financial Accounting Standards Board or FASB) increasingly focused on the content of the annual (and later quarterly) reports.

The standard annual report was the 10-K submitted to the SEC based on the SEC format, which included Management Discussion and Analysis (MD&A) and the financial statement section. Currently, corporations subject to SEC regulations (basically those listed on stock exchanges) must submit their 10-K to the SEC within 60 days of the end of the fiscal year. MD&A explains management's perspective of performance, financial condition, and future expectations. Included in MD&A is an extensive discussion of corporate risks and how the corporation manages those risks (especially the use of derivatives).

According to the SEC, four financial statements are required: the balance sheet, income statement, cash flow statement, and statement of equity (www.sec.gov/investor/pubs/begfinstmtguide.htm). The balance sheet summarizes the financial positions (assets, liabilities, and equity), while the income statement describes the major revenue and expense (plus gains and losses) categories to arrive at net income and earnings per share. The cash flow statement reanalyzes financial information from a cash perspective, separating cash from operations, investment, and financing. The equity statement provides additional information on changes in equity from stock issues, repurchase of shares (treasury stock), and other comprehensive income and losses (gains and losses recorded directly to equity rather than through the income statement, also called "dirty surplus").

Investors and other financial statement users have more faith in the accuracy of the annual reports, primarily because of the requirements of corporations to have a financial audit based on SEC requirements and to follow generally accepted accounting principles (GAAP). The FASB was established in 1973 as an independent organization (the previous two boards were under the American Institute of Certified Public Accountants (AICPA), the professional association of certified public accountants (CPAs)). Since 2009 accounting standard changes are made through the Accounting Standards Codification. Prior to the codification, the FASB issued 168 statements of financial accounting standards (SFASs) plus many other professional standards (interpretation, concept statements, staff positions, and so on). The current codification essentially represents a comprehensive summary of U.S. GAAP.

The format of the financial statements and the composition of the notes in the 10-K are primarily determined by SEC requirements and the FASB's codification. The first note generally is a summary of accounting principles used by the company topic by topic (e.g., describing the company and business segments, new pronouncements, revenue recognition, financial instruments). A large corporation may have 50 pages of notes and in some industries many more. Large business acquisitions are described in some detail; companies with defined benefit pension plans may have multiple pages of tables and descriptions; executive and employee compensation may be complex and also have detailed notes. And on it goes.

Users might get by with summary financial information (these are available online at sites such as Yahoo Finance). Alternatively, considerable information is available from the 10-K, 10-Q (quarterly report), other SEC reports, the company's website, and various finance Internet sites and other business media sources. For rather large fees, several huge data bases can be accessed for additional analyses. Unlike a century ago, there is no shortage of information, from raw data to detailed financial analysis.

Disclosure is critical in economic theory. Buyers and sellers (or agents and principals according to agency theory) have different amounts of critical information; usually, the seller has the relevant information useful for the buyers. Economists call this asymmetric information, which often leads to inefficient and sometimes disastrous decision making. Financial disclosures are one mechanism to reduce the information asymmetries between market participants. Of course, executives, and other participants with a vested interest in manipulation or other illicit activities have considerable incentives to hide or massage financial information.

Auditing

A textbook definition of auditing is as follows: "a systematic process of objectively obtaining and evaluating evidence regarding assertions about economic actions and events to ascertain the degree of correspondence between those assertions and established criteria and communicating the results to interested users."[1] Fundamentally, an audit firm reviews the financial information of the corporation based on formal audit standards to issue an auditor's opinion on whether or not the company conforms to GAAP. Thanks to the Sarbanes-Oxley Act of 2002, the audit firm also issues a report on the effectiveness of internal controls of the firm.

The audit profession was well established by 1900 and most of the original firms that became the "Big Eight" had been established in England or the United States. A century ago auditors typically checked every transaction: from the journal entry to the ledgers and back to every voucher or invoice; this was a simple, but time-consuming process. The point was to search for fraud and clerical errors. The audit role continued to expand as investors needed reliable information from major corporations and capital markets.

Audit regulations started in New York state, which first licensed CPAs in 1896. All states had licensing requirement for CPAs by the early 1920s. A national exam (the uniform CPA exam) started in 1917. In addition to state regulations, the majority of CPAs became members of professional societies (eventually the AICPAs became the most significant). There also were attempts to standardize both accounting and auditing practices. The Federal Reserve Board published *Uniform Accounting* in 1917, which basically standardized the audit process using a checklist for each balance sheet account and a standardized audit report.

A major source of new auditing standards came from audit results, with the failures the most noteworthy. An audit failure occurs when the auditor's report states the financial statements are unqualified (i.e., in accordance with generally accepted accounting principles), when, in fact, the financial statements are false or misleading. (A business failure, on the other hand, usually refers to bankruptcy.) The botched audit of McKesson Robbins in the 1930s, which did not uncover massive fraud, led to formal auditing standards established by a committee of the AICPA.

The use of the computer was perhaps the greatest business innovation of the second half of the 20th century, but it took decades for the audit profession to effectively audit around or through the computer. Of course, audit failures continued, as did continued regulations to overcome deficiencies. Sarbanes–Oxley, in response to the bankruptcies (and audit failures) of Enron, WorldCom, and the rest, included substantial regulatory changes, including the establishment of a new government-sponsored regulator, the Public Company Accounting Oversight Board (PCAOB).

What Are Accounting Manipulation and Fraud?

Fraud is defined as intentional deception for personal gain.[2] Accounting deception and fraud, the deliberate misstatement of financial information specifically for personal gain, has been a perpetual problem since the rise of capitalism. (Capitalism is an economic system with private ownership of production and distribution, with production levels determined by markets.) Cases of specific accounting fraud were not much of a criminal issue until accounting standards were established beginning in the late 1930s. Prior to that, with no established rules, what would now be called fraud and manipulation could be "acceptable accounting." Samuel Insull, infamous for utility stock pyramiding in the 1920s, was indicted for fraud in the early 1930s, but not convicted. The prosecutors could not convince the jurors that the illicit practices used were illegal or fraudulent. The first major accounting fraud of the accounting regulation era (since the Securities Acts of 1933–1934), did not take long. The on-going fraud of McKesson & Robbins, a large pharmaceutical company, was discovered (by an inside whistleblower, not the auditor) in 1938.

Corruption, on the other hand, the abuse of power or resources for personal gain ranging from deception and bribery to complex fraud, has a long and ignoble history. Corruption does not necessarily involve illegal acts, although corrupt activities are improper and unethical—with many successful scam artists operating on the edge between legal and illegal. As stated by business historian John Steele Gordon[3]: "nothing characterized American politics and thus the American economy so much as corruption." A scandal is a widely publicized incident that involves wrongdoing, disgrace, or moral outrage. Economic activity runs in cycles—the business cycle of expansions and contractions, bubbles, and busts. Corruption differs from scandals because it may be commonplace, unreported, or even the norm. Transparency International creates an annual corruption perception index by country, with the United States in an undistinguished 19th place—just beating out Chile. Certainly corruption is the norm in North Korea and Somalia—tied for last place at number 182.[4]

A distinction can be made between explicit corruption and legal corruption. Daniel Kaufmann, president of Revenue Watch Institute and Senior Fellow at the Brookings Institute, estimated that about $1 trillion is paid annually in bribes around the world—one form of explicit corruption. Legal corruption, according to Kaufmann, represents legal actions for private gain such as lobbying, campaign contributions, and the revolving door between regulator/bureaucrat and corporate manager/lobbyist. Kaufmann's index of legal corruption had the Netherlands with the lowest level of legal corruption (at 79.2) and the United States at a poor 30.8.[5]

Accounting manipulation is something of a special category. Companies are expected to "manage earnings," basically trying to achieve specific financial goals such as meeting a specific earnings target—having positive net income rather than a loss or meeting financial analysts' forecasts. Corporate executives have considerable discretion even in times of down earnings, such as reducing operating costs or lowering estimates of bad debts and hundreds of other reserves. On the other hand, company executives may be so desperate they are willing to commit fraud to achieve these ends. Enron had a not-so-illustrious history of doing exactly that, seemingly creating new categories of manipulation from one year to the next. It is difficult to determine how widespread illicit acts are within major companies or even the point at which earnings management becomes manipulation.

In an earlier book,[6] I developed an earnings management continuum from conservative accounting through fraud, with a few examples summarized in Table 1.1. Earnings management is an expected objective of corporate management. Corporation should consistently use conservative accounting, such as recognize sales only after the goods have been received by the buyer and title passes. However, incentives exist (including executive compensation based on accounting performance) that could encourage managers to use more aggressive accounting procedures to boost current-period earnings. If quarterly earnings based on conservative accounting are 24 cents a share and analysts' consensus earnings forecasts are 25 cents, the CFO can look for that extra penny, even if aggressive accounting is used. Based on Table 1.1, aggressive accounting and fraud can be considered earnings manipulation.

Why Do Companies Cheat?

According to Thomas Frank in *Pity the Billionaire*[7] "crime pays: Wall Street, we suddenly understood, had never been a reward for 'performance' or a grateful recognition of what financial innovation did for the nation—it was strictly about what Wall Streeters could get away with." More specifically: "(1) It pays to do it, (2) it's easy to do, and (3) it's unlikely that you'll get caught."[8] Basically, it is perverse incentives versus ethical standards and regulatory effectiveness.

Table 1.1. Earnings Management Continuum Examples

	Conservative	Moderate	Aggressive	Fraud
Revenue Recognition, Manufacturing	After sale, delivery and acceptance	After sale is made	Bill and hold	Fraudulent sale
Revenue recognition, services	Services prepaid and have been performed	Service prepaid and partially performed	Services agreed to, but not yet performed	Fraudulent scheme
Inventory	Lower of cost or market faithfully followed	Slow to write-down slow-moving inventory	Obsolescent inventory still on the books	Sham rebates on purchased inventory; nonexistent inventory
Accounts receivable	Conservative credit terms and bad debt allowance	Liberal credit terms and bad debts allowance	Liberalizing credit policies to expand sales and reduce bad debts by ignoring likely defaults	Fictitious receivables established to support nonexistent sales
Advertising, marketing	Expense as incurred	Expense based on some formula, perhaps sales-based	Marketing costs capitalized	Capitalized and manipulated to meet earnings targets; other costs treated as marketing and capitalized

Adapted from Giroux (2004), p. 3.

My first encounter with less-than-stellar business behavior came when I was a freshman in college. A friend, call him Steve, got a part-time job at a hardware store as a salesman. Early on, his commissions were close to zero and the owner almost fired him. Then the owner explained the rules. Steve's commission depended on the business making additional money—somewhat analogous to "economic rents" (basically excess profits). If the customer wanted an item that was advertised on sale, ring up the regular price; if the customer complains, apologize for the error and ring up the sales price. When a customer asks for help, refer him or her to the dogs, overstocked or overpriced items to get rid of. And so on. Steve got the hang of it and started bragging Monday mornings on his latest scam to generate increased commissions. This was my introduction into the real world of business, or at least one of the ugly sides of business.

Lesson one on business behavior: behavior follows incentives. Steve's incentives were obvious. If he wanted a commission, in fact if he wanted to keep his job, his boss demanded he cheat the customer. This ethically challenged policy was likely not a good strategy for long-run success of the hardware store, but that was not Steve's problem. The basic incentive structure was not that different from new employees at Enron in the 1990s. The facts can vary in thousands of different ways, but the outcome remains the same. Adapt to the system, whether ethical or not, or leave.

Consider the Enron case, perhaps the biggest accounting scandal ever, certainly one of the most written about. The public knows a lot about Enron, because so many insiders and journalists wrote books (my personal favorite was Kurt Eichenwald's *Conspiracy of Fools*). The Enron scandal proved personal for our accounting department at Texas A&M. David Duncan, Arthur Andersen's managing partner for the Enron audit, was a distinguished graduate of our program. He was a good guy, dedicated, a church-going family man, hard-working accountant rising to the top ranks of what was then a Big Six firm.

Andersen was indicted for destroying evidence, shredding documents related to the Enron audit. It was Duncan's decision (seemingly encouraged by top executives). As were many previous audit decisions allowing various aggressive Enron antics to continue. Duncan was fired by Andersen in 2002 and pled guilty to obstruction of justice charges. How was he caught up in this (at best) ethically ambiguous environment? I would not presume to know what specifically motivated him, but there was an obvious incentive structure and cultural environment. He had a prestigious job and was well-paid, apparently over $1 million annually. Andersen had a reputation for "aggressive auditing," approving procedures that another audit firm may have denied. Enron's culture certainly pushed the envelope on illicit activities, including pressuring auditors, attorneys, regulators, analysts, and banks to go along.

Lesson two involves regulations and regulators. Illicit behavior might be controlled if it is declared illegal, if the penalties are severe enough for perpetrators to take pause, and if the regulators actively enforce the law. The Securities Acts of the 1930s, for example, proved to be reasonably effective for decades and regulations were enforced by the relatively well-funded SEC. The same claim can be made for many if not most federal regulators. Effective enforcement involves well-written laws and regulations, adequate funding of agencies, dedicated leadership, and a culture of public service. Agencies can be crippled by changing regulations, reduced funding, and placing people in charge unwilling to enforce the rules (in part, associated with industries "capturing" the agency). There is pretty good evidence, for example, that the banking industry captured the Treasury Department and other banking regulators.[9]

An interesting question is to what extent government, and especially government regulators, take responsibility for fraudulent acts of corporations. In the Subprime Meltdown of 2008, at least hundreds of people committed illegal acts involving predatory lending and thousands of unethical (and perhaps illegal but never prosecuted) acts in the process of packaging mortgages into mortgage-backed securities and selling them around the world as AAA-rated securities—all with the blessing of the banking chief executive officers (CEOs). Alan Greenspan was Chairman of the Federal Reserve until he retired in 2006; in other words, during the development and peak of the mortgage bubble, which he encouraged in various ways and refused to regulate activities for which he had direct responsibilities. He committed no illegal acts, did not benefit financially from the mortgage bubble, and believed in what he was doing. Nevertheless, a case can be made that he bears more responsibility than anyone else for the catastrophe.[10]

Finding Cheaters

Incentives change over time; therefore, fraud and manipulation will also change. When foreign goods were taxed heavily during the 18th century, smuggling (transporting goods when prohibited by law) increased. When Prohibition outlawed liquor in the 1920s, organized crime moved in to provide illegal spirits. When tax rates went down in the post–World War II period (the top personal income tax rate was 91% in the 1950s and dropped to 28% with tax reform in 1986), executive pay exploded. CEOs in the 1950s wanted perquisites and other non-taxable benefits. In the 1990s and ever since, CEOs wanted stock options and big cash bonuses. Although they paid less in taxes, they wanted more income—much more. Because executive pay followed corporate earnings, "making the number" (increasing earnings per share based on rising analyst expectations) became job one—whether legitimate or not.

A basic assumption of financial analysis is predictions of future behavior of key actors can be made if the incentive structures are known. A good rule of thumb, for example, is to look at the compensation of the CEO and other top executives, which are detailed in the annual proxy statement. CEOs at companies with extremely high compensation levels, especially if they are not the largest or the most profitable in the industry, are more likely to engage in manipulation and unsavory practices. The premise is that an income-obsessed culture focuses on short-term profit over long-term performance, often with little if any interest in customers and other stakeholders. David Johnston[11] referred to electrical utility Entergy as just such a firm; J. Wayne Leonard was the highest paid CEO in the industry in 2008, while Entergy overcharged customers and skimped on infrastructure spending (including upgrading the electric grid). In other words, high billing rates but poor service. Entergy had plenty of competition: "Telephone, natural gas, water, and sewer utilities have been caught overcharging. ... According to a *New York Times* report in 2007, every fifth dollar the state of New York pays doctors, hospitals, and other providers is for care either not rendered or not needed."[12] The companies with the high-paid CEOs were the most likely to ignore high ethical standards.

In *Detecting Earnings Management*,[13] I focused on signals of bad behavior. An analysis using annual reports and other public documents can spot signals of manipulation, but not specific illicit events; that takes the inside information of an auditor, regulator, or whistleblower. Potential signals include companies that hand out excessive amounts of stock options and other forms of compensation and have large underfunded pension plans (extra unfunded pension plans for executives is a prime reason for overall underfunding). Companies can manipulate various allowance accounts—there may be hundreds of these on the books. Unfortunately, the only reserve account that companies must report is the allowance for doubtful accounts (related to bad debts of accounts receivable). Big changes in this account that don't match changes in receivables balances and sales are a potential signal. Presumably, if companies are manipulating this account, which is disclosed, they may be manipulating the hundreds of other allowance accounts big time.

The Big Scandals

The big scandals are those that make the history books, can be catastrophic to the economy, and often lead to increased regulation and oversight. Historically, the biggest and most disruptive scandals have been financial, usually after economic euphoria causing an asset pricing bubble and then the crash. The first recorded collapse was Tulip Mania in 17th-century Holland, literally over the love of tulips. The next century saw the South Sea Bubble and the Mississippi Bubble toppling the economies of England and France, respectively. The first American scandal was the Panic of 1792, when the country was exactly four years old. This involved the speculation of William Duer, a former Treasury official bidding up bank stocks based on insider information. His information proved to be wrong, he failed and went to debtors' prison, and the economy fell into a mercifully short recession.

19th-Century Scandals

The 19th century could be considered the first American century, with the United States rising from what today would be called a Third-World agrarian state to the industrial giant of the world. There was no secret formula, just a sundry cast of inventors, entrepreneurs, speculators, bankers, and assorted others building on a growing infrastructure and new ideas, within a relatively free market. The connivers were just as innovative as the inventors and entrepreneurs, but did not and had no interest in benefiting the public. A free market with few regulations benefits the crooks at least as much as the entrepreneurs.

Banks were chartered and regulated by states and each state was something of an experiment in finance. Relatively little regulation existed in many states, especially in the "wildcat banks" of the west. With banks issuing their own paper currency, a rising money supply periodically led to speculation, an asset bubble usually in real estate, and panics and depressions. Beginning with the Panic of 1819, major panics driven by speculation occurred about every 20 years plus various minor ones in between. The biggest banking event was President Andrew Jackson's ability to destroy the Second Bank of the United States in 1836 (essentially, America's central bank), which helped fuel the Panic of 1837.

A major development in government was the political machine associated with a political party within a city, county, or state. New York's Tammany Hall was the first, the most corrupt (but with plenty of competition), and the longest lasting. Aaron Burr's run for president in 1800 from his New York base introduced Tammany members to Burr's conniving political tricks. The Grand Sachems (the Tammany leaders) learned fast, including how to control votes, how to use patronage for power, and how to skim money from the city's taxpayers, business people wanting licenses and permits, and various job seekers. Police department jobs were for sale with the price going up from beat cop to captain. The biggest Tammany villain was William "'Boss' Tweed," the Grand Sachem after the Civil War. His level of corruption was so vast that he became one of the few 19th-century crooks actually sent to jail.

The major industry of the 19th century was railroading, getting its start in the late 1820s, becoming important by mid-century, and dominating the economy during the second half. Four major truck lines developed from the East Coast; the Pennsylvania became the biggest and developed many of the management and accounting techniques necessary for industrial success. The Erie proved to be the most corrupt, led and manipulated by speculators Daniel Drew, Jay Gould, and others. It would earn its epithet, "The Scarlett Woman of Wall Street." The great railroad scandals were Cornelius Vanderbilt's Raid on the Erie in 1868—he failed—and Credit Mobilier, the construction company building the Union Pacific half of the Transcontinental Railroad. Credit Mobilier involved stock payoff to politicians, which led to Congressional hearings, investigations, and indictments, but no convictions. Despite no slammer time for the culprits, it was still considered the biggest scandal of the century.

A multitude of scandals concerned the consolidation of industrial America by entrepreneurs such as John D. Rockefeller at Standard Oil and the Wall Street Bankers ("The Money Trust"), led by J.P. Morgan. To what extent these industrial leaders were heroes or villains has been hotly debated ever since. The success of industry concentration and growing monopoly power led to the Sherman Antitrust Act and other federal legislation to limit the powers of big business.

20th-Century Scandals

Although half the workers in the country still toiled on farms, America was an industrial giant by 1900 and many industries were big and dominated by a few firms. Monopoly power and related economies of scale became a key part of business strategy. After the Panic of 1907, the Congressional Pujo Hearings unearthed a whole host of illicit Wall Street practices of "the Money Trust" and various forms of stock manipulations. The 1920s became a decade of wanton abuses. This was the period of Charles Ponzi creating the infamous Ponzi scheme, the Teapot Dome scandal involving the federal government and oil tycoons, and a new set of Wall Street abuses. After the 1929 market crash the international match company Krueger and Toll failed and the Insull utility empire crashed, exposing additional fraud and corruption. By the end of the 1930s the McKesson & Robbins fraud exposed specific audit failures.

The post–World War II period brought economic success and new scandals. General Electric, Westinghouse, and smaller companies were involved in a government price conspiracy for turbine generators. For the first time ever, white collar criminals were sent to jail. The Penn Central Railroad went bankrupt after hiding information from investors and the public about the lack of liquidity, the biggest bankruptcy up to that time.

Conglomerates and other types of mergers were fueled by accounting manipulation, especially "dirty pooling," summarized by Abraham Briloff as "cleverly rigged accounting ploys" (CRAP). Michael Milken's junk bonds funded hostile takeovers and leveraged buyouts. A vast hostile takeover-insider trading-savings and loan scandal broke in the 1980s, sending Milken, Ivan Boesky, and others to jail and leading to the destruction of much of the savings and loan industry—requiring a federal bailout.

A multitude of derivative-related financial scandals started with the market crash of October 19, 1987. The market dropped 23% in a single day, with so-called portfolio insurance (a derivative play) the major culprit. Big derivative losses and scandals occurred throughout the 1990s, with the failure of hedge fund Long-Term Capital Management the major one. A mini-real estate bubble developed and popped in the 1990s, fueled by predatory lending and the start of structured finance. Apparently, the level of corruption and losses was not enough to actually cause new regulations or regulatory interest—that had to wait until the really gigantic real estate crash of 2008. A major financial scandal was Bank of Credit and Commerce International (BCCI), a global banking empire with a criminal corporate structure centered in Abu Dhabi, which collapsed in 1991.

Over the last half of the 20th century, several major frauds occurred at small companies. Equity Funding (1972) was involved in a computer fraud at an insurance company. ZZZZ Best was an insurance restoration company in the 1980s; its stock price growth was fueled by bogus restoration projects. EMS Government Securities defrauded Home State Bank of Ohio, in one of the few cases where a company bribed the auditor (a CPA) to cover up the fraud. Bigger corporate frauds occurred at the end of the 20th century. Rite Aid was a drugstore chain manipulating cost of goods sold, capitalizing operating expenses, refusing to write off obsolete inventory, and other accounting frauds. Consumer products company Sunbeam under a new CEO temporarily stayed afloat in the 1990s using aggressive and fraudulent revenue recognition and expense manipulation. Waste Management was another 1990s company with fraudulent accounting, including understating expenses, while violating environmental and antitrust laws.

21st-Century Scandals

It did not take long for major scandals to pop up in the 21st century. The tech bubble of the 1990s burst in 2000, followed by a whole series of accounting scandals: Enron, WorldCom, Adelphia, Global Crossing, Tyco, and others. Most were major failures at big companies, where the chief executives directed (or at least tolerated) the accounting fraud. All practiced long-term manipulation mainly to boost short-term earnings and stock prices to benefit executive compensation. It took the tech crash and recession to expose their misdeeds. Enron was the largest bankruptcy up to that time and likely was the major corporate fraud scandal in American history. Enron's failure sent shock waves throughout Wall Street and Washington; Congressional hearings were called almost immediately after Enron declared bankruptcy in December 2002. Legislation was written but languished in committee. Then WorldCom failed after an attempt to fraudulently misstate operating expenses amounting to billions of dollars. WorldCom became the new biggest bankruptcy and within weeks Congress passed the Sarbanes-Oxley Act reforming financial and accounting practices.

The major financial scandal of the century (and perhaps in world history) was the Subprime Meltdown of 2008, when investment bank flim-flam nearly brought down the world's financial economy. Mortgage lending and repackaging mortgages by investment banks created high-risk debt rated as investment-grade securities. Predatory banking practices and financial manipulations became increasingly widespread, with accounting fraud playing a secondary role. Major investment bank Lehman Brothers failed, Bear Sterns bought by J.P. Morgan in a "shotgun acquisition" with government support, Fannie Mae and Freddie Mac (government-sponsored enterprises created to guarantee and buy mortgages) seized by the feds and insurance giant American Insurance Group (AIG) and most major banks bailed out with federal funds under the Troubled Asset Relief Program (TARP). Despite a massive financial reform bill (Dodd-Frank), the wicked ways of the Wall Street banks continued.

Economics of Bad Behavior

Economists generally assume that humans are rational and selfish, and economic theory can certainly justify bad behavior. Even worse, this economic position seems to have the law on its side. Classical economic thought begins with Adam Smith's *Wealth of Nations* (1776), which incorporates free markets and laissez faire, plus the magic of the invisible hand, generally limiting government involvement in the corporate sphere to enforcing property rights. Neoclassical economics developed the formal economic models of pure competition and maximizing profits, assuming rational behavior, complete information, and other factors that made the models elegant but not realistic.

The role of regulation and free markets has been debated ever since, given centuries of incredible economic success, but also extreme examples of fraud, panics, and market collapse—not to mention safety and other worker-rights issues, environmental damage, and tax evasion. Unfortunately, regulatory failures abound and cognitive capture of regulators exists. What is an economist to think? Perspectives run the gamut from libertarianism to socialism, with libertarianism seeming to have the best arguments to justify potential corporate bad behavior.

Pragmatic Perspectives of the Robber Barons

Nineteenth century industry is filled with names of ruthless businessmen developing gigantic corporations and vast wealth. The typical claim of the barons, such as steel magnate Andrew Carnegie (who wrote about it) focused on ruthlessness as necessary to stay in business; giving in to social consideration (such as employee welfare) would result in higher costs, inability to compete effectively, and, ultimately, failure.

William Vanderbilt, railroad tycoon and son of Commodore Vanderbilt, famously stated: "The public be damned. I am working for my stockholders." Given that little financial information was provided and accounts seldom audited, it was not clear that stockholders were given that much consideration. Barons achieving monopoly power showed little regard for customers, such as railroads charging maximum rates to farmers and manufacturers delivering tainted foods and inferior products to customers. Timber interests, mining, petroleum, and chemical production decimated the environment, seemingly not of much interest to anyone except radical environmentalists, most notably future president Theodore Roosevelt, successful politician and bad businessman.

Employees typically were treated as another commodity. Wages, usually little above subsistence for unskilled workers in the best of times, often went down during depressions so companies could maintain interest and dividend payments. Worker safety was close to a non-issue as thousands of workers were killed each year and hundreds of thousands injured. Developing unions had little success, largely because governments enforced the property rights of business. Labor conditions periodically became bad enough to cause severe riots. Labor ultimately lost, but caused substantial economic damage in the process—both business and labor typically lost the public relations battle. Andrew Carnegie was a modest champion of labor rights; his contracts, for example, typically allowed salaries to rise and fall with the sales price of steel (in other words, about as close to a softy on labor rights as any robber baron can get). However, his name remains in labor infamy after the bloody Homestead Strike of 1892.

Business tycoons faced government officials on the take at every level, with extortion plans and bribes necessary to conduct basic operations. Progressive movements (political movements to provide social and economic reform) late in the 19th century resulted in governments becoming more of a friend to labor and the environment. Government corruption was reduced, although never eliminated. The role of government and regulation shifts over time, from periods favoring business (the 1920s) to period clamping down on business (the 1930s). The proper functions of rules and regulations continue to be debated, attempting to find the right balance of business versus public rights and responsibilities.

Social Responsibility Versus Libertarianism

Corporate social responsibility focuses on an ethical approach of executives to act in the best interests of all stakeholders: stockholders, creditors, customers, employees, and the public. Under this view, social responsibility is part of corporate governance and a major concern of the board of directors as part of the board's stewardship and long-term planning roles. The Business Roundtable developed a "Statement on Corporate Responsibilities" in 1981, including the potential benefits to reduce environmental activists and other nonmarket threats and various ethical considerations that could actually increase long-term profitability.

Libertarianism considers individual liberty as the greatest political good with only a limited role for government. This view is roughly consistent with Smith's laissez faire, although Smith had a somewhat greater role (and respect) for government. Noble prize-winning economist Milton Friedman was a proponent of libertarian economics and in an article conveniently called "The Social Responsibility of Business is to Increase its Profits,"[14] espoused that limited role of social responsibility.

The executive, according to Friedman, is the agent of the investors of the corporation and has the responsibility to make as much money as possible.

Friedman also notes that the company must conform to basic rules of society established by law and "ethical custom." However, Friedman makes clear that spending on, say, pollution control generally should not exceed that required by law. Of course, libertarians, with little regard for government to behave effectively, would oppose most of these regulations: "I share Adam Smith's skepticism about the benefits that can be expected from 'those who affected to trade for the public good'."[15] Thus, Friedman viewed social responsibility as a "fundamentally subversive doctrine."

Alan Greenspan, Chairman of the Federal Reserve (1978–2005), was a disciple of Ayn Rand, who preached objectivism, with many of the tenants of libertarianism. Despite bailing out Wall Street time and again (mainly because of the abuses of that most free market contract, the derivative), Greenspan was a believer in deregulation—an ironic perspective for the leader of one of the federal government's major regulators. He apparently believed that competitive banks and other corporations would regulate each other and ensure no fraud or other bad behavior happened. Thanks in part to his support, major deregulation bills passed, removing the separation of commercial and investment banks and effectively deregulating all over-the-counter derivatives. Greenspan's Fed also ignored the Fed's responsibility for financial consumer protections. These actions greatly assisted the creation of the subprime bubble.

The libertarian perspective in politics is alive and well, especially in the Republican Party. Proponents include the father–son team of Ron Paul (former Congressman from Texas) and Rand Paul (Senator from Kentucky). The basic mantra is cut taxes, cut spending, and cut government regulations.

Duty of Loyalty

In addition to economic theory, there is the corporate law duty of loyalty. Board members, executives, and other fiduciaries must act in the best interests of the corporation, not in their own interests. Self-dealing is out of the question. An open question is whether this requires them to promote profit maximization above all else. If so, public interest be damned. As stated by Rosenberg[16]:

> For decades, commentators and students of American business have accepted the basic premise that corporate leaders should make decisions that they reasonably believe to be "in the best interests of the corporation, with a view towards maximizing corporate profit and shareholder gain" and not to achieve any other social good.

Again, the interests of other stakeholders are not the concern of the executives and directors.

Leo Strine[17] looked to the courts on the importance of corporate stockholders. Early on, he talked about a famous 1919 case against Henry Ford (brought by the Dodge brothers, competitors of Ford and stockholders):

> Ford brazenly proclaimed that he was not managing Ford Motor Company to generate the best sustainable return for its stockholders. Rather, he announced that the stockholders should be content with the relatively small dividend they were getting and that Ford Motor Company would focus more on helping its consumers by lowering prices and on bettering the lives of its workers and society at large by raising wages and creating more jobs.[18]

Ford lost the case; the Michigan Supreme Court held "he could not subordinate the stockholders' best interest."[19]

Court cases continued. In a 2010 case eBay (once again, stockholder and competitor) sued Craigslist because Craigslist founder Craig Newmark focuses on a "community-oriented and community-driven corporation, not a cold-blooded profit-machine."[20] The court favored eBay and, once again, a cold-blooded profit machine. As summarized by Strine[21]:

> In the corporate republic, only stockholders get to vote and only stockholders get to sue to enforce directors' fiduciary duties. ... Precisely because it is ultimately the equity market that is the primary accountability system for public firms, efforts to tinker around with

the margins of corporate law through initiatives like constituency statues, the so-called Corporate Social Responsibility movement, and antitakeover provisions have been of very little utility in insulating corporate boards from stockholder and stock market pressures.

Extreme Cases of Bad Behavior

Perhaps the classic case to "defend" the economics of bad behavior is the Ford Pinto in the mid-1970s. The subcompact Pinto had this nasty habit of burning up in a crash. The answer according to the economics of profit maximization and duty of loyalty was cost-benefit analysis, which was actually conducted at Ford (based on an internal document later called "the Ford Pinto Memo"). The cause of the fires was a gas tank that could be punctured in a rear-end collision and, because of a lack of reinforcement between the rear panel and gas tank, the vehicle went up in flames. The cost to fix the problem was $11 per vehicle.

Fixing seems like a no-brainer, but it was not. Ford projected a number of deaths and injuries and multiplied these by expected damage (projected at $200,000 for one death and so on). That was the cost, compared to the "benefit" of saving 11 bucks per vehicle times the millions of Pintos expected to be sold. The conclusion was that the so-called benefits at over $100 million far exceeded the costs at less than $50 million. Ford was sued by crash victims in California and had to pay both compensatory and punitive damages in millions of dollars. (Juries were apparently swayed by Ford's brilliant cost-benefit analysis.) The actual number of deaths due to the design flaw was disputed, but hundreds of people died and Ford was forced to settle claims and eventually recalled the Pinto to fix the problem.

A recent example of corporate risk-taking was the British Petroleum (BP) *Deepwater Horizon* oil spill in 2010, caused by a wellhead blowout—the largest marine oil spill in history. BP had a history of taking shortcuts on maintenance and safety (30 workers were killed and over 200 injured in two previous disasters), a case study of corporate callousness and the focus on short-term profits over long-term risks. In 2012 BP pled guilty to 11 counts of manslaughter (for those dying at the Deepwater site), plus lying to Congress and other misdemeanors, with other cases still outstanding—total costs to settle this and other cases: over $40 billion. Strine[22] makes the case for bad behavior:

> It is to be expected that a corporation that stands to gain large profits from aggressive drilling activities would less than optimally consider the environmental risks and occupational hazards that novel drilling activity posed. BP, after all, stood to gain all the profits from its activities, while the risks to the environment would be borne largely by others.

In this perspective, the bankers and others responsible for the 2008 subprime meltdown do not seem evil; instead, they were pragmatic executives attempting to maximize short-term profits for shareholders.

The Role of Regulators

Regulations are the formal rules and requirements for controlling social and human interactions. Business rules have been on the books since ancient times and American regulations started from British precedents, common law, and colonial and state laws. The American Constitution split various responsibilities between the federal government and states with the federal government responsible for trade with foreign countries, coinage of money, and levying taxes. Most regulation of business was initially left up to the states. This worked reasonably well when commerce and travel were mainly local, but expanding business meant conflicting rules across states and the inability of states to deal with interstate commerce—a federal responsibility. Business regulation evolved from the dynamic patchwork of state and federal attempts at appropriate legislation, under judicial oversight. Businesses lobbied for regulations in their own interest, often against the public interest. The interests of politicians (getting reelected and often indulging in bribery and extortion—now called campaign funding) and regulators (initially patronage) were not necessarily in the public interest.

Economic-related regulations became increasingly important to meet the legitimate constituent needs. Rules change with new demands—often settled by lobbying effectiveness (which, early on, usually meant cash payments); regulations also go through periods of diligent versus lax enforcement for various reasons. When Britain increased and enforced regulations on taxes and trade after decades of lax enforcement, the result was the American Revolution. An interesting point is that lax enforcement are more likely during the boom times, partly because regulators do not want to disrupt prosperity—often encouraged by politicians on the dole from lobbying beneficiaries. New laws are put in place after economic collapses and the budgets and regulatory mandates expanded to increase enforcement (part of the "solution"). The most recent example was the Dodd-Frank bill of 2010, passed after the Subprime Meltdown. Bankers lobbied against the bill, then lobbied to reduce its effectiveness with both legislators and agencies writing and enforcing the provisions of the bill. Conveniently, banks (and other affected groups) often have lucrative jobs waiting for accommodating regulators and politicians.

CHAPTER 2

Business and Scandals before the Securities and Exchange Commission

Crises—unsustainable booms followed by calamitous busts—have always been with us, and with us they will always remain. ... The very things that give capitalism its vitality—its powers of innovation and its tolerance for risk—can also set the stage for asset and credit bubbles and eventually catastrophic meltdowns whose ill effects reverberate long afterward.

—Nouriel Roubini and Stephen Mihm

In 1789 as the nascent American government was being established in New York City, business-as-usual meant standard corruption practices like bribery and smuggling. Government had little involvement with business beyond chartering corporations and enforcing contracts and property rights. Manufacturing meant mainly handcrafted products, few banks existed before the Constitution was adopted, and financial markets were groups of merchants and speculators meeting on street corners or in coffee houses—something resembling Adam Smith's laissez faire state. Businesses were largely untaxed, while labor, safety, and environmental issues were of little concern to anyone in power. As the country's economy grew, banks got bigger and more aggressive, stock and other markets became formal and organized (under their own rules, not the government), transportation became rapid, efficient and more-or-less national, and the factory system developed and expanded. The American story is replete with stories of genius inventors (Eli Whitney and Thomas Edison come to mind), brilliant entrepreneurs (a big list including Andrew Carnegie and John D. Rockefeller), and financiers (with J.P. Morgan perhaps the most powerful). Lesser-known professional managers and accountants made plants run with increasing efficiency.

Without accounting or auditing standards, accounting fraud did not exactly exist, although massive manipulation and financial fraud were commonplace. During the railroad construction booms throughout much of the 19th century, promoters established construction companies to build the track and other infrastructure, charging the railroads outrageous prices. The promoters made a fortune whether the railroads were successful or not, or even if they were not completed. Bribes were common; cash accounting proved to be very flexible for the insiders. Fixed assets could be recorded at cost, some form of market value, or virtually any made-up number to benefit the managers and directors. Audits were often conducted, but the structure of the audit was completely at the discretion of the company treasurer or other corporate executives.

Businesses grew bigger and expanded across state lines. This created legal problems because of interstate commerce—limiting state laws (especially corporate charters) often made it difficult to operate in other states. Corporations turned to secret agreements and various illicit acts to circumvent legal restrictions. Intense competition prevailed, especially during economic downturns. This resulted in increased manipulation, bankruptcies, and attempts by the most ruthless to eliminate competitors or conspire to manipulate markets. The survivors were usually the most competent, innovative, and ruthless. (Having a war chest of cash did not hurt, either.) Survival and growth often meant skirting the law or worse (or, stated another way, extremely unethical behavior when few laws existed).

Governments got bigger and more corrupt. A good case can be made that Aaron Burr introduced the innovative tricks that transformed New York City's Tammany Hall from a social club to America's first political machine. Once Tammany's Grand Sachem's embraced machine politics government corruption increased on a massive scale (bribery and extortion became part of daily business) and expanded across the nation. For the most part, reform movements would have to wait until much later in the 19th century.

The post–Civil War period is known for the robber barons, a set of powerful and ruthless speculators and business leaders. Some were outright scoundrels, such as Jay Gould. Others were brilliant entrepreneurs interested in building mammoth enterprises, but not much interested in competitor welfare or public relations. John D. Rockefeller created the modern oil business, but became the number one robber baron for such maneuvers as secret railroad rebates, eliminating competition by any means possible, and using questionable legal wrangling to become a global enterprise. Rockefeller also was the most successful and efficient, becoming the nation's first billionaire. These "positive" characteristics are more appreciated today than at the end of the 19th century.

State laws attempted to regulate businesses of all kinds, basically dozens of experiments in business legislation. Some industries such as banks and insurance were often reasonably regulated. Others, especially large industrials, defied control, both because of effective lobbying of state governments and Article 1, Section 8 (on enumeration of powers) of the Constitution, which gives the federal government control over interstate commerce—reinforced by a number of Supreme Court decisions. After the Supreme Court decision in *Wabash, St. Louis and Pacific Railroad Company versus Illinois* of 1886 decimated the state's ability to regulate railroads, Congress finally acted, creating the Interstate Commerce Commission (ICC) in 1887 as a federal agency to do the job. Congress also moved to reduce the impact of corporate monopoly power. Three years after the ICC, the Sherman Antitrust Act began antitrust legislation to ban price conspiracies and limit monopoly acquisitions and power. Federal regulation has expanded ever since, in fits and starts, with the rule of thumb that major legislation followed mammoth scandals and crises.

By the start of the 20th century America was the global giant, overtaking England and Germany in production and industrial efficiency. Part of that success required accounting innovations allowing corporate headquarters to monitor and control massive operations across dozens of plants and distribution centers. The process continued with General Motors becoming the new innovative leader in manufacturing and accounting procedures by the mid-1920s. Unfortunately, the 1920s proved to be almost as corrupt at the late 19th century. This was the decade of Teapot Dome and Charles Ponzi. In addition, rampant speculation and manipulation fueled a market bubble, which burst in October 1929. A recession and stock crash turned into the Great Depression of the 1930s, largely because of misguided efforts by the Federal Reserve and other government actions.

The Founding and Early Business History

The Virginia Company, an English joint stock company (precursor of the modern corporation), established the Jamestown Colony in 1607, the first successful British settlement in what became America. Profitability came after the colony successfully exported tobacco back to the mother land. It would be followed by the Massachusetts Bay Colony, another joint stock company in 1620. The history books focused on religious freedom, and the stockholders focused on expected riches. Other colonies followed with similar capitalist expectations.

A million colonists scrounged around the original colonies by the 18th century. The South had the most people (with a substantial percent of those in slavery). Vast acreage of fertile land and warm weather made this an agricultural wonderland, exporting tobacco, rice, and indigo—cotton would become the big crop with the invention of the cotton gin and a nicely progressing Industrial Revolution in England. New England and the Middle Colonies (Pennsylvania, New York, and New Jersey) had poorer soil and weather, producing more limited foodstuffs. Their success came mainly from lumber, fishing, shipping, and merchandising. The North had the major port cities of Philadelphia, Boston, and New York City. The South had Charleston (New Orleans was a 19th-century acquisition from the Louisiana Purchase).

Britain developed a merchant empire with a big, expensive navy. The colonies provided raw materials and a market for finished goods. Colonists were expected to meet increasingly stringent mercantile regulations, pay customs, and other taxes (the system, especially with a big navy and frequent wars, was expensive) and be perpetually obedient to the king. The colonists, especially the merchant shippers, were good at evading taxes and regulations, with particular expertise in smuggling, bribery, and black market operations.[1] British taxes, regulations, and enforcement techniques became increasingly onerous after the French and Indian War ended in 1763, resulting in colonial unrest and disobedience. The Boston

Tea Party of 1773 was, perhaps, the most familiar act that led to the American Revolution (1775–1783).

The American hotheads likely did not think too carefully of the consequences of war with England when they declared independence in 1776. They initially had no government, no army or navy, no banks, no currency, and no means to raise money (the Patriots, after all, expressed a good deal of resentment to taxes). Not even half the colonists supported independence (together, British loyalists and fence-sitters were the majority). They were fighting the greatest professional military force on the planet, with the best banking and fiscal system available. Despite the long odds and substantial setbacks, the colonists triumphed.

With the war won, the provisional government under the Articles of Confederation was bankrupt, in debt, with few resources to reign in 13 independent colonies, and the country in depression. Shays Rebellion (1886–1887) of western Massachusetts (over onerous state taxes) was possibly the last straw and a group of political leaders from the colonies agreed to meet in Philadelphia to rewrite the Articles. The result was the American Constitution, written in 1787 and passed by the required nine states in 1788. America had a new government in 1789 under the first president, George Washington. The depression, no revenues, and massive debt became his problems. He was fortunate to pass the financial problems to his new Secretary of the Treasury, Alexander Hamilton, who created a long-lasting revenue source in custom duties, established the Bank of the United States that acted as a central bank, started a mint to coin money, and developed a process to assume the debts of both the Continental Congress and all the states. By the end of that century, the country had a well-funded, functioning federal government with a stable banking system, and substantial domestic and foreign credit. (If Moody's had been around at the time, the United States could have had an investment-grade rating even then.)

Despite the best efforts of Washington, Hamilton and a whole host of founding fathers, the country was still an agricultural backwater. Manufacturing, such as it was, was small, local, and labor intensive, mainly in textiles, sawmills, iron foundries, and grist mills. The factory system developed first in textiles, as it had earlier in England. Samuel Slater, an Englishman working as a superintendent in a textile factory, immigrated to New England and established the first American factory making yarn in the 1790s. Once the government, after a bit of lobbying, established high customs duties on British yarn and other textile products, New England textile mills exploded and expanded into integrated mills, producing all steps by machine. The growing size and complexity required sophisticated accounting, with material and labor cost information accumulated for each operating in the entire process and a limited attempt at measuring overhead costs.

Eli Whitney's 1793 patent for the cotton gin is one of the most famous patents in history, although dozens of people copied and sold cotton gins despite his court actions for protection. Ultimately giving up, he received a contract to produce 10,000 muskets for the Army (conveniently, his friend Oliver Wolcott was Secretary of the Treasury). The concept of interchangeable parts got a boost with Whitney's contract. He claimed to mechanize the process, but only developed part of the firing mechanism with interchangeable parts; the problem was lack of needed machinery. With improved machinery, interchangeable parts and mass production happened soon in firearms and spread rapidly across American industries. The Springfield Armory would introduce many firearm innovations and developed advanced accounting controls, considered the most sophisticated in use before 1840 according to Alfred Chandler.[2]

Banking and Financial Markets

When independence was declared, America had exactly zero banks thanks to a British ban on banking or minting money. Philadelphia financier and merchant Robert Morris (he became Superintendent of Finance for the Continental Congress) established the first commercial bank, the Bank of North America, chartered as a national corporation under the Continental Congress in 1781. It functioned as a conservative bank, taking in deposits, maintaining substantial reserves in gold, and issuing short-term commercial loans to established merchants (who still needed collateral for the loans). The bank also provided various central banking-type activities for the Continental Congress and Morris had substantial self-dealings with himself, the bank, and the government. These conflicts of interest would be illegal now, but were considered standard practice at the time.

Two other commercial banks were established in the 1780s, the Bank of New York by Alexander Hamilton and the Bank of Massachusetts by Boston merchants, both chartered by their respective states in 1784. Their practices were virtually identical to Morris's bank, maintaining conservative practices by keeping large reserves and limiting lending to short-term loans mainly to merchants. During the 1790s (after the U.S. Constitution created a dynamic federal government), another 26 banks were state-chartered, maintaining conservative practices (no American bank failed in the 18th century). As Treasury Secretary, Hamilton created the Bank of the United States in 1791 with a 20-year federal charter, modeled after the Bank of England to serve as a central bank. This was another link in Hamilton's chain to create a successful fiscal and monetary structure for the nation.

Washington considered himself politically nonpartisan, but before his term was over, Hamilton's Federalists were battling Thomas Jefferson's Democratic-Republicans for political and philosophical control. Under partisan politics, self-dealing became especially blatant. New bank charters won approval based on political party, with Federalists dominating the early banks. As leadership changed from one party to another, charters followed new party affiliation and government deposits transferred to party-affiliated banks. It was a short move from partisanship to political corruption. For example, New York City's Bank of America, the largest bank in 1815 with capital of $4 million, caused a scandal when Federalist politicians were accused of bribery over its charter.

The late 18th-century commercial banks played an important role at the start of the country by creating a stable and successful banking system, even though most people never used banks. The number of banks increased slowly, to 90 by 1811, and conservative practices continued through the War of 1812. A separate laboratory of corporate chartering and regulation developed in each state, with rules ranged from conservative, sound banking to virtually no regulation. Periods of paper currency explosions (banks issued their own paper money) was a sure recipe for banking and economic collapse. The result of "aggressive banking" was periods of rapid growth, expansion of services to farmers, retailers, and speculators. Some canal and railroad builders got initial funding from state banks. The downside was the creation of boom and bust cycles, causing havoc when banks and the economy collapsed.

Unlike urban banks, which tended to operate conservatively, rural banks, more common in the West, tended to be aggressive and often pegged as "wildcat" and "frontier" banks. Lower reserves, more risky loans funded with the bank's own notes, and a distaste for redeeming notes for gold generated quick profits. Bankruptcy often meant the bank promoters left town in the middle of the night to set up a new wildcat bank in another state.

Each bank produced its own notes in convenient denominations. The notes would be issued when customers took out loans. By mid-century, over 1,000 state banks operated, creating untold currency variations. With thousands of banknotes circulating, counterfeiting became rampant. Various reforms were tried by the states, including new, more stringent regulations and self-policing bank associations. Clearing banks were established beginning with the Suffolk Bank of Boston around 1819. Banks would affiliate with the clearing bank (usually by keeping deposits in that bank) if they wanted their notes redeemed. Some states instituted annual bank examinations, while others established bank commissions to supervise and examine the books of state banks. The result was a crazy quilt banking system, from conservative and stable in some locations to corrupt and risky in others (plus a ban on banking in a few—Texas did not have a bank until the 1860s). Generally, the further from the East Coast, the greater the hazards.

Politics and Political Machines

Political corruption could be found at all levels of government, but was particularly pervasive at the local level. The election of 1800 was a good start date for partisan, corrupt politics, a bitter fight between sitting President John Adams, a Federalist, against sitting Vice President Thomas Jefferson, a Democratic-Republican, and the rivalry filtered down to the local levels. Partisan newspapers supported a candidate and willingly told half-truths and lies about the opponent. New York lawyer and politician Aaron Burr was in the running for president as a Democratic-Republican. Burr could be considered a genius for political organization, especially when it involved dishonesty and fraud. He organized New York City Democrats to control the wards, used door-to-door arm twisting for vote getting and fund raising, lied to journalists using both partisan news-papers and bribery of reporters, and provided rides and other services on election day—this was before the secret ballot and henchmen could encourage "correct party voting."

The "Sachems" of Tammany Hall observed and expanded on the Burr tactics and Tammany became the long-serving base for the New York City's Democratic political machine, which specialized in power, corruption, and accumulating wealth by illicit means. William Mooney, an upholsterer and first Grand Sachem, paid himself grandly despite the allotted $1,500 a year salary and pilfered government goods ("trifles for Mrs. Mooney" was his defense). The vast potential for patronage jobs for Tammany sup-porters was first developed by John Ferguson, mayor of New York begin-ning in 1815. Tammany-controlled banks distributed stock to Tammany leaders. The Collector of the Port of New York, responsible for collecting tariffs, had the greatest bribery and embezzling potential and often ended in Tammany hands (when a Democrat was president). Collector and Burr ally Samuel Swartwout fled the country when an investigation exposed the embezzlement of $1.2 million of customs funds, followed by similar allegations of his successor as collector, Tammany boss Jesse Hoyt.

William (Boss) Tweed was considered the most corrupt Grand Sachem; his ring stole as much as $200 million. In part because of the infamous Tweed cartoons by Thomas Nast, Tweed was arrested and convicted in 1871, actually dying in jail in 1878—one of the few 19th-century crooks convicted of a crime. Corruption declined after Tweed, but neither Tam-many nor corruption went away. Political power and election success, with the resulting patronage, determined relative corruption potential. When Richard Croker became Grand Sachem in 1886, kickbacks and bribery returned, although more modestly than under Tweed. Croker's growing real estate empire benefitted from insider information and city-controlled property. Following the Tweed tradition (Tweed got Brooklyn Bridge stock, for example), Croker was given large stock holdings from companies wanting to do business in New York. The police department was blatantly set up for plunder and allied with Tammany—with at least limited reforms coming when Theodore Roosevelt became a police com-missioner and new Republican mayor William Strong started a reform movement in the 1890s.

Future president Martin Van Buren (1837–1841), who practiced law in New York City, maintained control of Democrats in New York State using political surrogates while in Washington; the "Albany Regency" was the first attempt as a nationwide political machine. The "Regency Code" used patronage as the primary technique to maintain power. Van Buren's increasing power in Washington made both state and federal jobs available. After the Civil War, Roscoe Conkling was the New York Republican machine boss competing with Tammany Hall. During the administration of U.S. Grant, federal political patronage and corruption was especially rampant. Teddy Roosevelt, a New York State Assemblyman about this time, referred to machine politicians from both parties as the "black horse cavalry." As a political reformer, Roosevelt was often stymied by the machines.

Chicago, America's number two city, was a late starter in machine politics, but became synonymous with corruption. Ward politicians blamed rivals for the Great Chicago Fire of 1871, soon transformed into the usual patronage and "vote early and often" campaigns. Democratic Michael McDonald created the first Chicago machine, followed by the Kelly-Nash machine. Prohibition increased the power of organized crime in Chicago politics. While most cities saw the decline of political machines in the 20th century, machine power actually increased in Chicago after 1930. The last major Chicago machine occurred during the reign of Mayor Richard Daley, starting in 1955. The other particularly infamous political bosses of the 20th century were Jersey City mayor Frank Hague and Tom Pendergast and his Kansas City machine. (Future senator and President Harry Truman came out of the Pendergast ring.)

Transportation: Canals and Railroads

Transportation proved to be a major obstacle to economic development. Initially, virtually all trade was done on water, across the Atlantic or down America's rivers. The major cities were the port cities of New York, Philadelphia, Baltimore, Charleston, and later New Orleans. However, except for available rivers, transport into the interior meant inefficient wagons and carriages. The first great building projects were canals, basically to connect cities to other cities or rivers that connected to other cities. The major issue was that the capital-intensive projects needed government support or capital markets to generate the funds for building. The early financial markets of, for example, Philadelphia and New York, initially funded government bonds, banks, and insurance companies.

Canals and later railroads required state charters, which needed political connections. The promoters of canals and railroads were a strange brew of idealists, politicians, investors, speculators, and various shady characters only interested in a quick buck. Many elites had the connections; promoters made connections with under-the-table cash. Many promoters sought to profit from the construction itself, whether or not the project actually succeeded as a business enterprise, called by critics "plunderers" and "looters." Despite the mixed incentives of the promoters, the canals and railroads got built. Promoters often sold subscriptions to stock shares, with a small percentage of the price up front and the rest payable over time. The best connected got government financing or other incentives such as blocks of land.

The first canal was the Santee Canal, built in 1792 from Charlestown, South Carolina, to connect to interior rivers. Even George Washington was a canal investor, the Patowmack Company to connect Alexandria, Virginia, to the Appalachian Mountains. By 1860 some 4,000 miles of canals were operating. The most successful was the Erie Canal, running from Buffalo on Lake Erie to Albany in the Hudson River, an easy jaunt by boat to New York City. The building was a political act and centered on the interests of those benefitting from the canal, including early steam boat operator Robert Fulton and New York land speculators. New York City mayor De Witt Clinton was the major political force behind the project—and the canal was dubbed "Clinton's ditch" by opponents. By 1822, some 220 miles were completed. Canal securities became favorites, first with New York elites and then English and other European investors. Cost overruns were a substantial 46% ($8.4 million vs. a project cost of $5.8 million); a later New York Congressional investigation committee named fraud as the major cause. Despite corruption, the canal was completed in 1825 and was a commercial success from the beginning, moving tons of grain, lumber, and later meat east and manufactured goods and immigrants west.

Railroads, beginning with the 16-mile Mohawk and Albany (from Albany to Schenectady) in 1831, became even more successful and a necessary engine for the rapid economic growth of the second half of the 19th century. The first of the successful major railroads was the Baltimore and Ohio Railroad (B&O), chartered in 1827 by Baltimore merchants to run from Baltimore to the Ohio River, basically to stay competitive with the Erie Canal. The route to Wheeling (on the Ohio River) was not completed until 1853.

Another major railroad was the Erie Railroad, chartered in 1832, running from near New York City to near Lake Erie (or, as the critics exclaimed, "roughly nowhere to nowhere"), for a short period the longest railroad in the world. Funding required common stock and, largely because of the high construction costs, a substantial amount of bonds. Many of these were convertible into stock (and some convertible in either direction). This was a speculator's perfect security and the Erie would prove to be among the most corrupt of the major railroads in U.S. history—the "Scarlet Woman of Wall Street."

Four major truck lines developed in the second half of the 19th century. In addition to the B&O and Erie, they included the New York Central (beginning around New York City, it took a route roughly parallel to the Erie Canal and later headed west to Chicago and beyond) and the Pennsylvania Railroad (from Philadelphia to Pittsburg and beyond). The rise of professional management and cost accounting developed in the railroads, with the Pennsylvania taking the lead. The railroads were a mixed bag, with professionalism and a focus on near-lifetime employment at some like the Pennsylvania, while corruption and short-term speculation dominated others, like the Erie.

The big railroads developed top-down management structures because of their size and operating complexity. Profitability when competition and high fixed costs existed required the movement of maximum traffic most efficiently. In addition to professional management, this required substantial improvements in accounting. As summarized by Chandler[3] "To meet the needs of managing the first modern business enterprise, managers of large American railroads during the 1850s and 1860s invented nearly all of the basic techniques of modern accounting."

The Pennsylvania Railroad divided the traffic into three separate companies, each headed by a general manager and J. Edgar Thomson serving as president of all of them. Under Thomson a uniform set of accounts and reporting system was put in place and many operations, such as purchasing, was handled at the central office for maximum economies. The standard measure of performance was the operating ratio (operating revenues divided by operating expenses) to compare volume efficiency. Another common measure was the ton mile as a measure of unit cost, developed by civil engineer Albert Fink, then general supervisor at the Louis & Nashville Railroad.

The Big Scandals

In a century with few regulations, it was difficult to commit criminal acts related to complex business dealings. Many outright frauds of today would have been considered standard practices, such as insider trading, market manipulation, self-dealing, and any number of conflicts of interest. Also, basic frauds such as bribery and extortion were typically overlooked, partly because both judges and legislators were often on the take. Both labor and the environment were often treated harshly, with only limited regulation for their protection by the end of the century. The concept of worker rights did not exist and thousands of workers were killed on the job and perhaps hundreds of thousands injured annually. Despite these caveats, many business scandals occurred. The major scandals included raiding the Erie, the attempted gold corner of 1869, and the Credit Mobilier scandal. Interestingly, these occurred about the same time—Boss Tweed also was being prosecuted about then.

Raiding the Erie

Cornelius Vanderbilt moved from a steamboat fleet to a railroad empire. He sold his ships and achieved effective control of the New York Central by the mid-1860s. His biggest frustration was the conniving at the Erie, manipulated by speculator Daniel Drew. Vanderbilt wanted a well-functioning railroad; Drew wanted to manipulate Erie's stock. That meant he could push to stock price up or down and also start rate wars with the New York Central and Pennsylvania Railroad. Vanderbilt could form a price/volume agreement with the Pennsylvania (basically a cartel), but not the Erie (Erie's managers would agree to a plan and then cheat). Vanderbilt's answer: acquire the Erie. He had to deal with Daniel Drew and his co-conspirators Jay Gould and Jim Fisk. In this major battle involving millions of dollars, Vanderbilt would lose—a rare event. The war included an attempted corner, newly printed Erie securities, accommodating judges willing to subvert justice and bribing politicians.

Drew had served as an Erie director since 1851 and later treasurer; manipulating Erie stock proved to be his most lucrative endeavor. Drew made a successful bear raid in 1866 (driving down the stock price by selling short and using other mechanisms to reinforce a lower stock price) and using Erie's convertible bonds to cover his short position. Vanderbilt's Erie raid started soon after. He accumulated enough stock and proxies to gain control. Drew, still Treasurer and claiming to be a Vanderbilt ally, planned a counter-strategy.

Drew's lobbying resulted in a new state law allowing railroads to exchange stock to acquire other railroads under lease. Drew leased the rundown Buffalo, Bradford, and Pittsburgh, for $9 million, paid for with Erie convertible bonds; $5 million worth went to Drew's broker and these were convertible into 50,000 shares of stock. Vanderbilt was frantically buying the newly minted stock. Once alerted they were brand new shares, Vanderbilt got judge (and Tammany member) George Barnard to issue a restraining order on these activities, but Drew used his own judge to countermand the order and compel the Erie to convert the bonds. Judge Barnard countered with contempt proceedings against Drew, Gould, Fisk, and other Erie directors. Soon to be called the Erie Ring, Drew and his conspirators fled to New Jersey with all the newly acquired cash.

The Erie Ring used their Albany forces to entice the state legislature to introduce a bill legalizing the new stock and forbid consolidating the Erie with the New York Central. Vanderbilt's cash bought enough votes to defeat the bill. A similar bill was introduced in the Senate (Gould was leading the Erie forces in Albany at the time) and the bill passed. The house legislators expected a massive payoff in a new round. But Vanderbilt had had enough, sending this message to Drew: "I'm sick of the whole damned business. Come and see me. Van Derbilt."[4] Vanderbilt sold his stock back at less than he paid for it and withdrew completely from the Erie—Drew and his co-conspirators won. Gould and Fisk proved even more mendacious than Drew, driving him from Erie management. Gould proceeded to loot the Erie once again, until finally ousted in 1874, leaving a ruined railroad declaring bankruptcy the following year.

The Gold Corner

Gould and Fisk were soon at it again, this time attempting to corner the gold market in New York City. Because much of the city's gold was sent west in the summer and fall to pay for the annual agriculture harvests, that was the time to act. The plan could succeed only if the federal government did not make Treasury Department gold available to the market. Bribery of corrupt government officials was part B of the plan. The result of the corner would be much higher gold prices, devaluation of greenbacks (the paper currency of the time), and inflation. The rationale was that inflation would benefit the farmers; the harm to merchants and consumers was ignored.

Gould and Fisk, still running the Erie, used the railroad's cash to buy gold, selling $2.5 million in Erie stock to generate the cash. About $4 million in gold existed in the New York market. The Treasury Department controlled another $15–20 million in gold. The Treasury must be kept out of the market. The plan was to bribe President U.S. Grant's brother-in-law Abel Corbin. Corbin arranged a meeting between Grant and Gould at Fisk's theater where the "gold plan" was explained, focusing on the benefit to farmers. Grant agreed, telling Treasury Secretary George Boutwell not to interfere.

Gold stood at $130 (130% of the value of greenbacks), when Gould and Fisk started buying. Corbin, in the meantime, demanded more cash, which was not forthcoming. Fisk and Gould had also offered General Horace Porter, Grant's private secretary, a bribe, which he turned down. Porter told Grant about the bribe. An outraged Grant changed his mind and ordered Boutwell to break the corner. Gould discovered the Treasury action, sold out, and made millions. Gould neglected to tell Fisk, who continued to buy gold, sending gold over $160. When Boutwell announced the gold sale, the price of gold almost immediately fell back to $130. Fisk should have been ruined, but refused to pay. His brokerage firm defaulted and went bankrupt. Lawsuits followed, but Gould's judges protected Fisk. Congressional hearings investigated the gold corner. When Fisk was called his answer was: "Nothing is lost save honor."

Credit Mobilier

The first transcontinental railroad ran from Nebraska to California, finally linking the country from coast to coast. Federal legislation passed during the Civil War and construction completed in 1869, considered by many the most spectacular building project of the 19th century. The multiyear construction resulted in perhaps the biggest scandal of the time, Credit Mobilier. The basic corruption was well known from other railroads, but the scale and the number of corrupt federal officials getting caught was unique.

Many visionaries, including Abraham Lincoln, favored a transcontinental railroad. The discovery of gold and the mass rush of the "forty-niners" made it inevitable. To entice promoters still required a government giveaway of millions of acres of federal land and millions in federal loans. More enthusiasm was generated in California where the Central Pacific Railroad (CP) was chartered by the state in 1861, financed by four merchants, Leland Stanford, Collis Huntington, Charles Crocker, and Mark Hopkins. Called "the Associates," they were interested in long-run money and power, which limited their immediate pilfering. Theodore Judah, the initial visionary and creator and surveyor of the railroad, died of yellow fever in 1863.

The Pacific Railroad bill was passed by Congress in 1862 and provided both substantial loans and land, based on miles of track completed. The bill created the Union Pacific Railroad (UP) as a federal corporation with Union general and New York politician, John Dix as president. Thomas Durant, a Wall Street speculator, was appointed as vice president and became the real driving force. In total, Congress loaned the two railroads $51 million and 21 million acres of land. The promoters of both companies would sell much of the land though separate land companies; the proceeds went to the railroads only after the promoter's substantial cut.

Corruption extended beyond Washington. After extensive "lobbying" in Washington the CP had virtually no money for construction. The CP associates developed an extortion racket, including a suggested "subsidy" from cities on the potential route; if they wanted to be on the route, funds were expected. Sacramento, San Francisco, and Stockton were three California cities paying up: cash plus right-of-ways, land, and other benefits. A favorable press required appropriate payments: the *Sacramento Union* editor reputedly received $3,600 worth of CP stock and reporters lesser sums.

The major public scandal centered on the construction companies established by each: Credit and Finance Corporation used by the Central Pacific and Credit Mobilier (CM) at the Union Pacific. The CP associates and Durant of the UP secretly ran the construction companies and, along with influential politicians and other insiders, owned the stock. George Francis Train, hired by Durant to sell UP securities, found a "shell company" in Pennsylvania and suggested the name Credit Mobilier of America (after a French company). Durant and Massachusetts Congressman Oakes Ames became the major stockholders of Credit Mobilier. Durant did not expect the UP to succeed and wanted the opportunity to make his fortune up front by skimming off as much money as possible through the construction company.

The two construction companies acquired the supplies and completed the construction—either directly or through subcontractors. General Grenville Dodge was the chief engineer of the UP and under his efforts Credit Mobilier profits were massive. Big dividends were paid no matter what, resulting in Credit Mobilier doing a poor job actually paying suppliers, workers, and subcontractors. Associate Charles Crocker ran the CP construction company. He served as president and the four associates owned all the stock, camouflaged by using phony investors. The CP construction company certainly made big profits, but the amount is unknown: when Congress subpoenaed them, the books "mysteriously disappeared."

Somehow both railroads got built, meeting at Promontory Point, Utah, on May 10, 1869. Then the scandal broke. Congressman Ames had sold stock of both UP and Credit Mobilier to influential politicians as low prices (buyers included vice president Schuyler Colfax; James Blaine, Speaker of the House of Representatives and later senator, presidential candidate, and secretary of state; and James Garfield, Speaker of the House and later president). An 1872 article by Charles Francis Adams, Jr. called

"The Pacific Railroad Ring" broke the story, which demonstrated the massive corruption and obvious conflicts of interest: "the members of it are in Congress; they are trustees for the bondholders; they are directors; they are stockholders; they are contractors; in Washington they vote the subsidies, in New York they receive them, upon the plains they expend them, and in the 'Credit Mobilier' they divide them."[5]

The Adams's story was followed up by a *New York Sun* investigation, which called Credit Mobilier "The King of Frauds: How the Credit Mobilier Bought Its Way Through Congress." Congress held hearing, creating the Credit Mobilier Committee. The press dubbed Congressman Oakes Ames "Hoax Ames." Ames was accused by Congress of stock payoffs, lying to Congress, and massive overcharging of the UP for construction costs. In 1873 Congress censured Ames, who died soon after. Ames had acquired enough shares to push Durant out of CM leadership and Durant escaped almost untouched because he was ousted by Ames in 1869.

None of the perpetrators was prosecuted. The Justice Department did sue Credit Mobilier for fraud and expropriation of funds but the Supreme Court ruled in favor of the company. The railroad eventually repaid the federal debt when it became due decades later, but only after losing in court. Gould acquired the UP in 1873, looting it and driving it toward bankruptcy. The CP continued in the hands of the associates, who continued to expand their giant land and railroad empire, dominating California for the rest of the century.

Industrialization and Monopoly Power

During the 19th century, the United States rose from an agrarian economy to an industrial giant, outstripping both Britain and Germany for manufacturing dominance. America had a unique system of government, banks and capital markets, entrepreneurs and inventors, and the development of a class of professional managers. The earliest factory systems were New England textiles mills, using British models of machinery. The big business for most of the 19th century was the railroads, where efficiency, coordination, timing, and vast information needs led to professional management and improved cost accounting. According to Livesay,[6] "modern bureaucratic management structures [were created] because they had no choice. Their size and complexity precluded the use of traditional methods of finance and management." The railroads moved massive amounts of goods and people, which required the lowest possible cost if the company planned to stay in business. This required the best information available. As stated by Chandler,[7] "to meet the needs of managing the first modern business enterprise, managers of large American railroads during the 1850s and 1860s invented nearly all of the basic techniques of modern accounting."

The Pennsylvania Railroad was perhaps the most innovative railroad, especially under the presidency of J. Edgar Thomson (1852–1874): "Thomson was indeed one of the most brilliant organizational innovators in American history."[8] Andrew Carnegie trained on the Pennsylvania Railroad and used his accumulated knowledge to create and run the gigantic Carnegie Steel Company. After viewing Henry Bessemer's steel plants in England, Carnegie created a steel manufacturing partnership in 1872 using the Bessemer process. He was confident, backed by his understanding of management and finance and the need for steel rails by the Pennsylvania and other railroads. His accounting system was the best available, using a voucher system to accumulate labor and materials cost for each department and prepare monthly reports. His plants were so efficient that he could operate at near capacity at a profit even during depressions. He sold out to banker J.P. Morgan as part of the consolidation movement working through most industries.

Industries producing complex but relatively homogeneous products could achieve substantial economies of scale with size; with market dominance the major firms could control pricing and limit the entry of new competitors. This, according to the proponents, created stable markets and promoted quality products. The critics claimed monopoly power, outrageous prices, and lack of innovation. The benefits of economics of scale were too attractive for big business to ignore. Consolidations meant horizontal mergers with competitors, vertical mergers to reduce costs, and ensure availability of supplies and distribution channels. The increased complexity required sophisticated accounting and reporting mechanisms through a professional central office. J.P. Morgan and other members of the "Money Trust" consolidated railroads and dozens of other industries, including Carnegie Steel as part of Morgan's massive United States Steel, capitalized as the first billion-dollar corporation in 1901. The Sherman Antitrust Act of 1890 and additional legislation attempted to eliminate the worst abuses of consolidations, price fixing, and monopoly power by big industrials.

Panics and Crashes

The business cycle measures the ups and downs of the economy from expansion to bust to recovery and another expansion. The country was in depression when the Americans won the revolution and created a new government. Recovery followed George Washington into office, only to be hit by the first downturn (Panic of 1792) within four years. During the 19th century, major panics and depressions occurred about every 20 years (1819, 1837, 1857, 1873, and 1893) with minor downturns in between.

Various economic theories have been posited, with the Minsky Model, taking a broad historical perspective, a particularly useful starting point. Economist Hyman Minsky (1919–1996) focused on investor confidence and the supply of credit, resulting in changing bank lending practices and relative quality of debt: hedge finance (safe), speculative finance (moderate), and Ponzi finance (risky). The key point is that under standard conservative banking practices, interest and principal payments will likely be paid back on time. As speculation begins and then euphoria takes over, riskier lending occurs, which is unlikely to be paid back when asset prices fall and the economy turns down. The point when asset prices collapse is the "Minsky Moment"—Holland tulip prices in 1637, South Sea Company stock in London in 1720, Wall Street stock prices in 1929, American real estate in 2007.

Brunnermeier and Oehmke[9] expand on the Minsky model to analyze financial crises. In their view, there are two phases: (1) a run-up phase where bubbles form and (2) a crisis phase resulting in a crash. During the run-up asset prices rise, rationalized by innovations (based on, say, railroads, the Internet or financial innovations such as securitization). Consistent with Ponzi financing, easy credit drives up asset prices beyond fundamentals, the creation of investor euphoria—a bubble, fueled in part by "belief distortion." A trigger event leads to crisis, such as a price drop in key assets, followed by amplification mechanisms such as bank runs and lack of further credit.

The first major 19th century panic and crash was the Panic of 1819. Numerous state bank charters led to over-borrowing, causing speculation and rising prices in land and securities. Also in 1819 was a $4 million payment in gold due to the Barings Bank (President Jefferson borrowed the money for the Louisiana Purchase of 1803). The Second Bank of the United States (essentially the central bank of the time) called in state bank notes it possessed, demanding payment in gold. A ripple effect collapsed the domestic money supply. Credit essentially stopped and borrowers (fundamentally speculators at this "Ponzi stage") failed in mass. Prices collapsed, banks failed, bankruptcies were widespread, and a major depression was underway.

The Panic of 1837 had many similarities to the earlier Panic of 1819, with too many banks making risky loans, and land speculation driving up prices. The unique events were the roles of President Andrew Jackson and European markets. The textile industry in Britain collapsed, decreasing foreign trade and reducing cotton and other commodity prices. Jackson's government required specie payments (gold and silver) to purchase public lands, which quickly destroyed land prices. Speculators defaulted, banks failed, and the panic was on. Jackson did not renew the charter of the Second Bank of the United States, which could have limited the damage caused by the panic. With no central bank, a major depression set in—after Martin Van Buren replaced Jackson as president. Van Buren took the blame and was destined to be a one-term president.

Just like clockwork, the Panic of 1857 occurred 20 years after the last, with railroads playing a big role for the first time. After gold was discovered in California, new gold and silver finds increased the supply of specie, driving up inflation and asset prices. The Crimean War of 1853–1856 increased farm exports. The euphoria led to massive railroad construction and speculation in farmland. When the Crimean War ended exports and grain prices collapsed, ending the boom. The immediate cause of the 1857 panic was the failure of a New York trust company, causing bank runs and investors pulling out of securities. Hundreds of the railroads expanding roads using borrowed money failed, as did thousands of other businesses. The depression was short, because of the impending Civil War.

Railroads would play a major role in the remaining two major panics of the 19th century. With the completion of the first transcontinental railroad in 1869, others followed. Jay Cooke took over the Northern Pacific Railroad, relying on cheap credit. Unfortunately, much of his financing depended on German and Austrian speculators. When the Vienna Stock Exchange collapsed in 1873, so did Jay Cooke and Sons. This forced the closure of the New York Stock Exchange (NYSE) and the failure of a multitude of overextended railroads and banks. The depression that followed lasted the rest of the decade.

The Panic of 1893, following the booming decade of the 1880s, resulted in possibly the worst depression of the century. Once again, railroads were overleveraged after massive construction projects (total miles of track doubled during the 1880s). The immediate cause of the panic was the bankruptcy of the Philadelphia and Reading Railroad and the National Cordage Company, after a declining money supply and falling exports. Panic set in as investors cashed out to acquire gold; 150 railroads failed including the B&O, Erie, UP, and Northern Pacific. Also falling were 500 banks and thousands of other businesses. Recovery began in 1896, but the economy stayed in the doldrums throughout the decade.

The Panic of 1907 was caused by an attempted corner of a copper company. The broker involved failed, resulting in a general Wall Street panic and the collapse of the Knickerbocker Trust Company. With other trusts and banks in jeopardy, J. P. Morgan stepped in to bail out much of Wall Street. Morgan's actions reduced the severity of the collapse, but later Congressional (Pujo) hearings uncovered many financial abuses on Wall Street. One result was the creation of the Federal Reserve System in 1914 and additional business regulation.

Anything-Goes-1920s and the Great Crash

After eight years of Democratic control under Woodrow Wilson, the nation returned to Republican rule in the 1920s, lower taxes, reduced regulations, and a hands-off federal government. The economy boomed, especially in the second half of the decade and considerable innovation happened (automobiles, electric utilities, radio, and airlines were the high-tech industries of the age). The speculation-fueled stock market boomed, creating a classic euphoria—destined for the Great Crash before the end of the decade. This was also the decade of perhaps the greatest government-business scandal, Teapot Dome, and Charles Ponzi, the namesake of the infamous scheme.

Teapot Dome

Teapot Dome in Wyoming was one of several naval oil reserves (the other major ones were in California). The scandal involved a large cohort of corrupt politicians, businessmen, and administration officials out to buy a president and rig leasing (with big bribes) to oil drillers— despite all the substantial reform legislation of the previous 30 years. If corrupt Attorney General Harry Daugherty is included, it could be considered the worst scandal in American history.

Oilman Jake Hamon plotted to buy a Republican president in the 1920 election for $1 million. In return, Hamon would be named Secretary of the Interior, where he would sell oil rights to the federal oil reserves for big payoffs. The offer was accepted by presidential dark horse Ohio Senator Warren G. Harding[10] through his campaign manager (and Ohio party boss) Harry Daugherty. Hamon's plan was successful and Harding was elected president. Harding's wife insisted Hamon give up his mistress Clara. Mistress Clara did not take the news well and shot and killed Hamon before he assumed his role as Commerce Secretary. Hamon's conspirators Harry Sinclair, Edward Deheny, and Robert Stewart, all oilmen, demanded the plan continue. Instead of Hamon, New Mexico Senator Albert Fall became Interior Secretary. After appropriate bribes (Deheny gave Fall $100,000 in cash and Sinclair gave Liberty bonds—Treasury bonds issued during World War I—worth about $270,000), the plan went forth.

Sinclair and Deheny signed leases for the government's Teapot Dome and California reserve oil. Reporters for the *Denver Post* uncovered much of the Sinclair-Fall scam. Instead of disclosing the fraud, they demanded a bribe of $1 million from Sinclair. When he refused, stories about the conspiracy began and continued until they got their million bucks. Fall resigned after renewing the Teapot contract and became a "political consultant" for Sinclair and Deheny.

Once allegations began appearing in the press, Congressional hearing were demanded and started under Montana Senator Thomas Walsh in late 1922. As the perpetrators were covering their tracks, Walsh (and later the Secret Service) investigated. Deheny did admit to the $100,000 "loan" to Fall. The Liberty bonds were easy to trace because they had serial numbers. Criminal indictments for fraud were filed against Fall, Sinclair, Doheny, and others. Fall was convicted, making him the first cabinet officer to be jailed for a felony. He served nine months in prison and paid a $100,000 fine. Doheny was tried on the same issues but acquitted. Eliminating the drilling proved difficult. Sinclair beat the Teapot Dome charges but was convicted for contempt of Congress for lying and jury tampering.

The new attorney general filed injunctions to void the leases and stop the drilling at the naval reserves. Despite the massive evidence of fraud, it took a Supreme Court ruling to void the oil reserve leases in 1927.

Montana Senator Burton Wheeler (a protégé of Walsh) investigated Attorney General Harry Daugherty on multiple grounds. Daugherty brought much of his Ohio Gang to Washington—all thugs. The Bureau of Investigation (later the Federal Bureau of Investigation) became Daugherty's enforcer. Kickbacks were received from contractors to the Veteran's Bureau. Permits were sold to organized crime to sell alcohol (this was during Prohibition). Pardons and paroles could be bought by jailed criminals. Based on the building evidence, President Coolidge fired Daugherty in 1924. Lawsuits against Daugherty were filed, but he was never convicted.

The Ponzi Schemer

Charles Ponzi (1882–1949) was a crook in Italy, migrated to America as a crook, spent some time in a Canadian jail for fraud, and returned to the United States to promote his infamous scheme. A Ponzi scheme is a scam claiming big returns for investors, but paying off early investors from the cash of later investors. Because no real earnings exist, the scam must collapse sooner or later. Ponzi's gimmick was international reply coupons, which could be exchanged for postage stamps to a foreign country. Ponzi discovered that the coupons had different prices in various countries, partly because of fluctuating currencies. Coupons purchased in bulk in one country could be sold in another at a profit. That was his story. He established a company in Boston in 1920 claiming to pay investors 50% interest in 45 days or 100% in 90 days. Ponzi paid his early investors the huge return and investors flocked to his door.

Unfortunately, the coupon scheme could not work on a large scale. There was no cash return. The post office gave out stamps, not money; Ponzi's scheme required millions of coupons. Ponzi's major problem was increasing attention. *The Boston Post* investigated, followed by the Boston District Attorney, the state Attorney General, U.S. District Attorney, and the state bank examiner. The District Attorney arrested Ponzi, who pled guilty to larceny and mail fraud.

Ponzi was a small-time crook and his scheme defrauded relatively few investors. However, Ponzi schemes occur regularly and can be sophisticated and long-lasting. The most successful was Bernard Madoff, defrauding investors of billions of dollars over decades, caught because of his own cash squeeze in the 2008 financial debacle.

Market Manipulation and the Market Crash

By the 1920s, Wall Street was the financial capital of the world and the NYSE the biggest securities market. The NYSE had 61% of all American securities transactions in 1929. It was established as a private club to promote the interests of its members, not the public. Among the NYSE members were floor traders (trading only for their own accounts) and stock specialists (making a market in specific stocks, but without any limits on how they could profit from the stock). Conspiracies with other members could lead to stock pools to manipulate stock prices, including long-standing techniques such as wash sales (selling among themselves to drive prices up or down), naked short selling (selling stocks they did not yet own), and bear raids to drive down prices to cover short positions. The insiders profited, outsiders took the losses.

Despite the manipulation, high commissions and other charges to outsiders, the stock market boomed, especially in the last half of the decade—fueled by speculation and margin trading (buying stocks mainly using high-cost credit called broker loans). Brokers profited both on commissions and interest. Margin buying magnified both capital gains and losses, increasing volatility. Even small price drops could trigger margin calls, requiring buyers to cover their losses with cash or the broker would sell the stock—making market declines worse. Because corporate financial information was considered private (the rationale being that disclosure could benefit competitors), corporations could manipulate, misrepresent and conceal relevant financial data. With virtually no standardization of accounting or financial disclosures, dividends were the primary investment focus.

Prior to federal securities laws and regulations, the corporate culture could be deceptive, with little concern for underlying risks. Insider trading was legal and regularly practiced. Investment bankers sold new securities at discount prices to "preferred list" customers before the stocks were available to the public. Stock pools, syndicates established both within and outside the stock exchanges, manipulated stock price—100 or more stocks were openly rigged. The Chase Bank chairman sold his own stock short during the 1929 crash, using money borrowed from the bank. The president of the NYSE would later be convicted of embezzlement. Various bank executives would be charged with income tax evasion.

A few safeguards existed, including some state regulations, legal reviews on new issues, and various stock exchange regulations. Voluntary audits were conducted by about 90% of NYSE firms, but the audit scope was determined by the corporations being audited. The prospectus issued by investment banks for new securities was typically no more than four pages and written by lawyers mainly to protect bankers from potential lawsuits. The Federal Trade Commission, Internal Revenue Service (IRS), and other federal regulatory agencies had additional requirements. Taken together, there appeared to be considerable regulation; however, few if any rules had real teeth—a recurring theme.

The crash happened in October 1929. The Dow Jones Industrial Average (Dow) peaked at 386 on September of 1929, up over 500% from its 1920 low. Stock prices at that level averaged a very high 30 times earnings (a price to earnings or PE ratio of 15 is about average). As the economy slipped into recession (industrial production peaked in June, 1929), stock prices started dropping.

By October 23, the Dow dropped to 306, down 20% from the September high, triggering margin calls. The next day, Thursday, October 24, became Black Thursday, with morning sell orders causing a panic. A consortium of banks under J.P. Morgan agreed to support the market and Richard Whitney, the NYSE vice president representing the consortium, bought thousands of shares of about 20 stocks. The panic stopped for the day. But the following Tuesday, Black Tuesday, was a disaster (and no bank consortium stepped in). The Dow dropped 13.5%, the worst day in Dow history until 1987. By mid-November, the Dow was down almost 50%. The Dow would keep plunging until mid-1932, dropping almost 90%.

Lessons to be Learned

The first 300 years of America was a series of experiments in commerce and establishing the right balance of government and institutions claiming to benefit constituents. Budding entrepreneurs proved to be good at evading debilitation rules. As regulations expanded (created primarily by democratic means), business people continued to exploit favorable rules and avoid or evade difficult ones. Corruption was matched by innovation. Progressive reformers introduced stricter regulations and the response was greater efforts to exploit loopholes and minimize the perceived damage. Whatever the institutional framework, incentives drove behavior. Fortunately, there are limits to corruption. Given democracy in action, property rights, and the rule of law, the long-term results were economic growth, the rise of the middle class, and, eventually, world economic dominance.

CHAPTER 3

Great Depression and Reforms

To me, the issue of transparency is really about deception. ... But markets on their own seem not able to provide the proper amount of transparency, which is why government has to step in and require the disclosure of information.

—Joseph Stiglitz

Following the complete collapse of the U.S. economy and the discovery of massive manipulation and several large corporate scandals, the 1930s brought in Franklin D. Roosevelt's (FDR) New Deal and federal regulation of markets and corporations. Of particular importance was the creation of the Securities and Exchange Commission (SEC), which developed rules of corporate accounting and financial disclosure. The SEC was given control over accounting procedures, which were ultimately delegated to the private sector, with the American Institute of Accountants (AIA, now the American Institute of Certified Public Accounting, AICPA) assuming the responsibility. The largest and most successful auditing firms evolved into the "Big Eight." Beginning with New York in 1897, all states had a formal licensing process for certified public accountants (CPAs). In the process, accounting become more formal and supported by a growing profession. Accounting manipulation and fraud could now be defined with reasonable accuracy. It did not take long for the first major criminal fraud case to materialize, McKesson & Robbins (MR), a large pharmaceutical company.

The Great Depression

Although the U.S economy was already in recession, the market crash of October 1929 is usually considered the start of the Great Depression, a decade-long economic catastrophe. Banks failed by the thousands and millions of investors, large and small, investing heavily on margin lost it all—Groucho Marx being a famous example. Most individuals lost all faith in the market and stayed out of stocks for decades.

President Herbert Hoover continued the Republican pro-business stance of the 1920s and "traditional approaches" for dealing with economic slumps, including raising taxes and bailing out some businesses. Hoover's Treasury Secretary Andrew Mellon, one of America's richest men, famously declared: "liquidate labor, liquidate stocks, liquidate the farmers, liquidate real estate … purge the rottenness out of the system"—not a philosophy to promote government action (or reelection of Hoover). The unemployment rate, 2.9% in 1929, rose to 22.9% by 1932, while gross domestic product plunged 43% (from $104 billion to $59 billion).

Congress got into the act of smashing the economy with the Smoot-Hawley Tariff of 1930, which increased tariffs, bringing retaliation and decimating foreign trade. Because of rising federal deficits, Congress passed the Revenue Act of 1932, raising tax rates (with the top income tax rate rising from 25% to 63%). These blunders were considered responsible fiscal actions at the time.

Initially, the Federal Reserve provided positive action as the New York Federal Reserve under George Harrison lowered interest rates and flooded cash into the banking system. Unfortunately, the Federal Reserve Board in Washington supported Mellon's call for higher interest rates. Fed action mandated by Washington drove Treasury bill rates from 3.2% to 3.7% to maintain the U.S. gold supply and value of the dollar (mainly by selling Treasury securities to decrease the money supply). Economist Milton Friedman claimed this action was the primary cause of the Great Depression. Banks failed by the thousands.

FDR won the 1932 presidential election, then faced a banking crisis on his first day in office, March 4, 1933. The New York Stock Exchange (NYSE) closed the same day because of the banking crisis. The market opened two weeks later and went up after dynamic actions by FDR. The Dow hit 100 by July 1933 and rose as various New Deal programs appeared reasonably effective. The Dow peaked at 194 in March 1937. After that, the market and the economy headed down on a combination of poor monetary and fiscal policy actions, resulting in a recession in the middle of the depression. At the end of the 1930s, the Dow was back to 150 but economic recovery had to wait until World War II.

Business Scandals and the Pecora Commission

Typical of a bursting economic bubble, the depression of the 1930s resulted in the discovery of widespread corruption, fraud, and scandals. Kreuger and Toll (KT), a Swedish multinational with a major U.S. focus, was a complete fraud. Holding company pyramiding (multiple layers of companies usually in a specific industry based on huge levels of leverage) proved to be common during the 1920s and led to bankruptcy in the 1930s. Samuel Insull ran a utility pyramid, which failed, and he was indicted for fraud. Investment trusts, holding companies selling debt and equity securities to the public, often on large margin, lost vast sums of money for their investors.

Pecora Commission

In 1932, the Senate Banking and Currency Committee investigated the market crash and depression, which became the Pecora Commission, named for Ferdinand Pecora, the last chief council of the Senate committee. The common view of the crash and depression (shared by President Hubert Hoover and much of Washington) was the deceit of short sellers and Wall Street: "Hoover now shared the average American's view of Wall Street as a giant casino rigged by professionals."[1] Richard Whitney, NYSE president and first witness (more on him shortly), proclaimed the virtues of Wall Street, especially the NYSE. The hearings dragged on until Pecora became chief council (the fourth) early in 1933. According to Chernow[2]:

> With Pecora as counsel, the hearings acquired a new, irresistible momentum. They would afford a secret history of the crash, a sobering postmortem of the twenties that would blacken the name of bankers for a generation. From now on, they would be called banksters.

Speculators testified about their manipulations, including Harry Sinclair (jailed for his involvement in Teapot Dome) and Bernard ("Sell 'Em Ben") Smith. Techniques included stock pools to manipulate prices, insider trading, and bribing of journalists to influence prices. The income tax records of Wall Street bankers were analyzed, including the tax-avoidance schemes at J.P. Morgan (Morgan partners, for example, paid no income tax in 1931 and 1932) and other banks. Several executives were indicted for tax evasion, including Charles Mitchell, president of National City Bank, the largest bank at the time. Banks repackaged delinquent bank loans from South American countries as bonds, selling them as "low-risk government debt." Albert Wiggins, president of Chase National Bank, shorted the bank's stock using money borrowed from the bank.

Pecora investigated the many scandals of the era, including the stock pyramiding schemes in utilities (with Samuel Insull's empire prominently) and the Van Swearingen brothers and others in railroads; the KT fraud; and leveraged investment trusts. U.S. Attorney General John Sargent indicted over 1,500 firms and individuals, and conducted almost 150 criminal prosecutions. The Internal Revenue Service (IRS) collected about $2 million from tax evasion fines based on Pecora testimony. Pecora became a commissioner of the SEC after it was created.

Kreuger and Toll

KT was a construction and engineering company founded in 1908 by Ivar Kreuger and Paul Toll. It was split in to two with the holding company KT run by Kreuger. KT invested in various industrial companies, using Swedish Match Company as the base. Kreuger became involved in numerous complex international dealings. KT acquired various European match companies, using large-scale production, emphasizing economies of scale and increased efficiency in both production and distribution. KT eventually became the largest match company in the world.

International agreements at the time involved bribery of key officials and KT became increasingly corrupt. Archibald MacLeish[3] thought 1923 was the year Kreuger became an outright crook, creating International Match Company (IMCO) when the match industries ceased being profitable. KT used loans to European governments for favorable deals, including France in 1927 for a match monopoly. Early in the 1930s KT controlled over 200 companies and continued to pay large dividends, suggesting that Kreuger was one of the richest and most powerful entrepreneurs in the world. However, his empire was a composite of legitimate businesses and smoke. Bookkeepers relied on numbers supplied by Kreuger to create financial statements and move cash and other assets around the globe—mainly to issue new securities to raise the cash from U.S. and Swedish investors to keep the empire alive. Ultimately, even forging Italian securities was not enough to keep the empire afloat during the depression. Kreuger shot himself to death in 1932, creating what became the "Kreuger Crash," as KT and related securities collapsed—transforming Kreuger from the "match king" to the "world's greatest swindler."

Understanding the fraud and settling accounts took over a decade. Price Waterhouse audited the books and stated that the KT balance sheet "grossly misrepresented the true financial position of the company."[4] The American operations of KT failed in 1933. The Pecora Commission investigated KT and the forthcoming securities regulations were based in part on the financial failings of KT. Some of the KT empire survived, including KT Construction (which changed its name to Toll Construction). The final report was issued in 1945, resulting in bond holders receiving 30¢ on the dollar.

Samuel Insull and Stock Pyramiding

Samuel Insull created a utility empire that proved highly successful based on stock pyramiding, but failed in the Great Depression. He started working for Thomas Edison shortly after Edison invented the light bulb and electric generation, becoming a vice president of Edison Electric. A competent manager, he became president of Chicago Edison, transforming it into Commonwealth Edison in 1907. Insull formed Middle West Utilities as his first holding company in 1912, acquiring small, inefficient local utilities—the strategy was reducing costs, increasing efficiency, and growing the customer base.

He created Insull Utility Investments in 1928 as his pyramiding base, using high leverage to expand. Stock price exploded, from the initial public offering price of $12 to $150 within six months. Insull Utility created five holding companies under his umbrella and these owned over 100 separate utilities. At the height of the stock bubble in 1929, this empire had a market capitalization of $3 billion, with profits largely generated by writing up the value of property, plant, and equipment, while ignoring various operating expenses. Stock dividends from subsidiaries also were treated as income. Insull Utilities went bankrupt in 1931—one of over 50 failing holding companies. Insull was charged with mail fraud and antitrust violations and fled the country. He was extradited back to the United States, stood trial, but was not convicted. Without specific accounting standards, a jury was not convinced fraud had occurred. The illicit methods did not seem to violate any existing laws.

Goldman Sacks Trading

Investment trusts became a new tool in the 1920s, promoted by investment banks as the new innovation of financial engineering for small investors to reap the rewards of professional management. They resembled later mutual funds but without the regulations. According to a *Time* article in 1929, basically at the top of the market[5]:

> The investor in an Investment Trust, in effect, turns his money over to a group of experts who have the advantage of thorough market knowledge and of handling sums ranging from three to five hundred million dollars. Such an investor is letting men like Simon William Straus, the Seligmans, Arthur Cutten, Fred Fisher, and Walter Chrysler, invest his money for him. Investors in U.S. investment trusts usually do not know exactly where their money is being used (English investment trusts are more considerate); they are simply trusting the Trust. Perhaps the best analogy to an Investment Trust would be a hypothetical bank that had no restrictions on what it could do with the depositors' money. Funds invested in Investment Trusts may well yield 10% or more, may also yield nothing at all. Prior to 1925 there were only 29 U.S. investment trusts; at present there are some 200.

Goldman Sachs was a latecomer, but Goldman Sachs Trading Corporation (GSTC), not created until 1928, became the biggest and riskiest. GSTC started with little capital, but soon increased to $100,000 (with 10% retained by the Goldman partners, about half the equity of the partnership). GSTC zoomed to $326 a share (three times the initial price) just before the 1929 market crash—in part driven by trading shares to drive up the price. Based on GSTC success, two new investment trusts were formed by Goldman, both using substantial leverage.

When the market collapsed in late 1929, GSTC fell, bottoming out at $1.75 (less than one percent of its high). The holding company barely avoided failure, selling the remnants to Atlas Corporation in 1932. Goldman almost went under, but managed barely to survive the depression and World War II. None of the investment banks did well, nor were they or their services appreciated by the public.

Richard Whitney

Whitney was the NYSE executive who "saved the day" on Black Thursday, buying thousands of shares of several stocks as prices were collapsing. Of course, the market collapsed a few days later anyway. Whitney, as NYSE president, was the first witness of the Pecora hearings, proclaiming the benefits of the exchange. Unfortunately, Whitney had a dark side that would send him to jail.

Whitney and his brokerage firm, Richard Whitney and Company, were ruined by the crash, but hid the fact by borrowing money using his company stock as collateral for loans (because the firm was private, he was able to hide the fact that the stock had no value). He also borrowed money from his successful brother George (a partner at Goldman Sachs) or anyone who would lend to him. That was not enough to maintain his lifestyle, so he resorted to embezzling. As a trustee of the NYSE Gratuity Fund (basically a life insurance fund for members), he sold about $1 million in bonds in the Fund's name and kept the cash. He was also treasurer of the New York Yacht Club and looted the club. When caught, he confessed to brother George who loaned him $1 million to cover the crime.

Whitney's total debt was a staggering $27 million when the crime spree came to an end. His brokerage firm was suspended and New York District Attorney Thomas Dewey indicted Whitney for grand larceny. FDR famously exclaimed when he heard the news: "not Dick Whitney!" Whitney pled guilty and served about three years of a five-to-ten year sentence. That was the end of his less-than-illustrious career on Wall Street.

FDR and the New Deal Reforms

Roosevelt was New York Governor when Hoover was president. As governor he experimented with a number of welfare and work programs similar to those he later used as president. FDR easily beat Hoover for the presidency in 1932 promising a New Deal of reform of the banking system, unemployment relief, and economic recovery. New federal securities statutes were a major New Deal promise. On inauguration day, March 4, 1933, facing a complete collapse of the banking system and NYSE, which had closed, FDR declared a national "bank holiday," shutting down all banks until they could be inspected to determine which were still solvent. Solvent banks were reopened under the supervision of the Treasury Department and loans became available from the Reconstruction Finance Corporation (RFC)—over the next six months the RFC loaned out about a billion dollars. Despite this effort, 4,000 poorly capitalized and mainly rural banks failed. This was the beginning of the "first hundred days" of landmark legislation, part of FDR's first New Deal when 15 major bills were passed. The strategy was economic stimulation and massive financial and economic reform.

The primary bank reform bill was the Glass-Steagall Act of 1933. The act created the Federal Deposit Insurance Corporation, which insured holders of commercial bank deposits. Although insurance was not favored by FDR (who thought it propped up weak banks to the detriment of strong banks—a moral hazard according to economists), it was popular with constituents and remains a major regulatory agency. Based on a number of banking scandals, Glass-Steagall required the separation of commercial banks from investment banks. Scandals considered included the reissuance of failed bank loans to Latin American countries as government bonds sold to individual investors, the failure of investment trusts, and the multitude of Wall Street abusive practices. J.P. Morgan, for example, became a commercial bank, while Morgan Stanley was split off as an investment bank.

Stabilizing farm prices was an early New Deal focus. The Agricultural Adjustment Act (May 1933) was designed to raise agricultural prices by subsidizing farmers to reduce output, later declared unconstitutional by the Supreme Court. The program was modified and agricultural subsidies and related farm programs have been around ever since. The net result was to increase prices, good for farmers but bad for consumers and taxpayers.

One of Roosevelt's pet projects was the National Industrial Recovery Act (NIRA), passed in June 1933, which created the National Recovery Administration to eliminate "cutthroat competition" by establishing a cartel system of businesses and labor. Somehow, this collusion was supposed to result in "fair competition." In practice, the critics contended that it was particularly unfair to small businesses and promoted monopoly practices of large corporations. The Supreme Court ruled the law unconstitutional as a violation of antitrust laws. In its place, Congress passed the Wagner Act, greatly increasing the power of labor unions.

Many programs were launched as relief efforts, beginning with the creations of the Federal Emergency Relief Administration (actually a modification of an act passed during the Hoover Administration), which gave some $3 billion in grants to state and local governments to employ millions of unskilled workers. It was replaced by the Public Works Administration, which spent over $13 billion on public works between 1935 and 1943, with highway spending being the largest category. The Civilian Conservation Corps was another public works program (1933–1943), specifically hiring unemployed, unmarried men from relief families at $30 a month ($25 of which went to the parents).

A "Second New Deal" represented reform legislation to solve more long-term problems. The largest and most well-known was the Social Security Act of 1935, providing annuity retirement payments, disability, and other programs. The concept was a self-funding program paid from payroll taxes. Although payroll tax collections started in 1937, the first payments were not made until 1940. Problems did not develop for decades, until life expectancy substantially increased. The Federal Housing Act (FHA) provided housing-related loans. The FHA created the Federal National Mortgage Association (Fannie Mae) in 1938, another program that worked well for decades, until corruption and "housing euphoria" essentially bankrupted the company during the housing crisis of 2008. The Communications Act of 1934 established the Federal Communication Commission to regulate electronic communications, initially radio and telephone services. The Wagner Act (National Labor Relations Act) also was a Second New Deal program.

Roosevelt's programs were only partially successful. Some worked well, such as Social Security; others, such as the NIRA, were ruled unconstitutional. Many programs, especially the relief programs were often underfunded and later cut or eliminated. The federal government ran a deficit every year of the 1930s decade, increasing the political pressure to raise taxes and cut spending. The individual income tax was increased, with the top rate rising to 79% in 1936, as was the corporate tax rate, to 39%. Also, in 1937, the Federal Reserve reduced the money supply, causing a recession within the depression. Ultimately, the Great Depression ended only with World War II.

The SEC and Accounting Standards

The untold corruption and scandals associated with the market crash and unregulated business practices of the 1920s led to substantial reform including federal regulations and formal accounting and auditing standards. This proved to be a slow and evolving process, with major deficiencies often discovered after scandals and new issues created by a changing business environment. Central to the process was the SEC, which was given federal responsibility for accounting and disclosure practices.

Securities and Exchange Commission

After the market crash, the collapse of the banking system, and the findings of the Pecora Commission, most Americans lost all faith in the financial system. The answer, according to Washington, was the federal regulation of financial securities, including initial issues and the stock exchanges, replacing the ineffective state ("Blue Sky") laws. The original legislation was the Securities Act of 1933, also called the Truth in Securities Act. The banking industry lobbied to stall or reduce the effectiveness of the act, but to no avail. It was "the rare time when money talked and nobody listened."[6] A major focus was the need for full disclosure of relevant financial information. The Federal Trade Commission (FTC) was responsible for regulation under this act.

The 1934 bill attempted to improve securities regulation relative to the 1933 Act. It created the SEC specifically to regulate securities markets.

The mission of the SEC was (and still is) "to protect investors, maintain fair, orderly, and efficient markets, and facilitate capital formation" (www.sec.gov). Five Commissioners, each serving five-year terms, head the agency. Joseph P. Kennedy, a market manipulator during the 1920s and father of President John F. Kennedy, was the first Chairman of the SEC (1934–1935). The rationale was it took a speculator to understand and prevent illicit practices ("takes one to catch one," according to FDR).

Certain abuses identified by Pecora including margin trading and short selling; floor traders were banned from buying and selling exclusively for their own accounts. Legislation required the SEC to study each of these issues, which ultimately led to new regulations. Margin trading, for example, was not eliminated but the percent of leverage was limited. Other perceived abuses were studied by the SEC but not eliminated, including the use of preferred lists for initial public offerings.

The Securities Acts mandated "full and fair disclosure" of financial data in registration statements before a public offering, including the information needs of a "prudent investor." Legal requirements and antifraud provisions increased legal risks to corporations and bankers. Section 10b set the antifraud provisions of the 1934 Act. The SEC's Rule 10b-5 prohibits any "device, scheme, or artifice to defraud." The rule specifically restricts earnings manipulation, price fixing, and insider trading. In addition, the corporate is liable for any misstatement or omission of material facts.

The SEC required public corporations with over $5 million in assets and 500 stockholders to register with the regulator and file periodic reports before new securities could be issued to the public; exchange-listed companies had to file annual financial statements and other reports with the SEC. An annual audit was required for all trading corporations, making the auditors legally accountable to the SEC (also called "the public") in addition to the corporation audited.

The SEC's Regulation S-X lays out the format and required content of the various financial reports, available on the SEC's website at www.sec.gov/about/forms/forms-x.pdf. Accounting Series Releases (ASRs) issued by the SEC are official accounting pronouncements on accounting and auditing procedures required for reports issued to the SEC, such as the 10-K. These are codified as Financial Reporting Releases. Staff accounting bulletins (SABs) are interpretations and policies used by the SEC staff (of the Corporate Finance Division) on disclosure requirements. Well over 100 SABs have been issued, which are codified by topic at www.sec.gov/accounts/sabcode.htm. Other SEC documents related to accounting issues include accounting and auditing enforcement releases to detail misconduct of companies and/or auditors after SEC investigations.

In the pre–World War II period, the SEC was well-funded, with a staff of over 1,700. During much of the post–World War II period, budget cuts reduced agency effectiveness. Examination and inspections were often postponed. The relative aggressiveness (and budget level) depended on the specific administration in power, with Democratic administration often more assertive than Republicans. Lax enforcement typically meant increased probability of corruption and fraud undetected for long periods. One reason that major scandals such as Enron went undetected until the tech collapse of the early 21st century, was because of lax SEC enforcement—funding was increased with the Sarbanes-Oxley Act of 2002.

Accounting Standards

Prior to the creation of the SEC there were no formal accounting standards and not much interest in standardizing accounting and financial reporting. Many corporations considered finances a private matter and did not disclose any financial information. Until 1910, the NYSE had an "unlisted department" of securities from corporations refusing to disclose any information. Accountants typically emphasized the importance of judgment in determining how balance sheet accounts were valued, when and how much to recognize in revenues, and how to match expenses with revenues recognized.

The Interstate Commerce Commission, the federal agency regulating railroads since 1887, developed a uniform system of accounts for railroads (various states had earlier uniform accounting standards for railroads and other industries). Consequently, the concept of accounting standards for business was not out of the question. Accounting failures were noted after the Panics of 1893 and 1907. The Bureau of Corporations was established in 1903 to investigate business affairs. The Pujo Hearings of 1912–1913 uncovered many abuses of the "Money Trust" and big business. The FTC was created in 1914 to protect consumers and prevent anticompetitive business practices—the Bureau of Corporations was collapsed into the FTC. In 1917 the Federal Reserve, FTC, and AIA published "Uniform Accounting" in the *Federal Reserve Bulletin* to increase standardization of accounting disclosure and auditing methods. Because compliance was voluntary, this attempt had little impact on either financial reporting or auditing. According to Hawkins,[7] "In the area of prospectus financial disclosure the impact of 'Uniform Accounting' was almost nil."

In 1933 the NYSE required all listed firms to disclose audited financial statements and partnered with the AIA on accounting and audit issues. This private sector action was beneficial, but comprehensive reform had to come from the federal government. The SEC had Congressional authority to regulate accounting and disclosure with: "Authority … to prescribe the form or forms in which the required information shall be set forth, the items or details to be shown in the balance sheet and the earnings statement, and the methods to be followed in the preparation of accounts."[8] The Chief Accountant of the SEC from 1935 to 1938, Carman Blough, did not believe the agency had the resources to establish accounting standards. The SEC implicitly transferred the authority to the AIA based on ASR No. 4 (1938), which gave the organization with "substantial authoritative support" the responsibility.

The AIA created the Committee on Accounting Procedure (CAP) in 1938 to issue what became generally accepted accounting principles. The process was ad hoc, created by this part-time committee of accountants; however, the results proved reasonably effective and the CAP issued some 51 Accounting Research Bulletins (ARBs) over the next 20 years. Most of the basic accounting procedures came in large part from these ARBs—first codified in ARB No. 43 in 1953. Deficiencies of the CAP would lead to new committees, but the fundamental process of establishing accounting standards in the private sector was established. After the accounting abuses associated with fair value techniques of the 1920s and 1930s, both the CAP and IRS favored historical cost accounting rather than fair value measures.

MR and Audit Reform

Before the Great Depression, financial auditing practices were not standardized and substantial abuses could be hidden based on the limited scope of some audits or the deficiencies in audit techniques used. Both Insull Utilities and various subsidiaries of KT were audited, but were inadequate and helped camouflage the widespread corruption. Abuses were uncovered before the Pecora Hearings (in part by additional audits), which analyzed both fraud cases. The NYSE called for annual audits and SEC rules later required audits conducted by CPAs. This was a boon to the accounting profession, but before the 1930s decade was over a major fraud was discovered, perpetrated at a company audited for years by the premier accounting firm, Price Waterhouse.

McKesson & Robbins

MR was an old, established pharmaceutical company originally founded in 1833. MR was acquired by Frank Coster in 1927. Unfortunately, Coster (his real name was Philip Musica) was a crook and con artist who also happened to be a good business person—if he had been honest, MR could have been increasingly successful even during the depression. Before acquiring MR, Musica ran Girard and Co. as a pharmaceutical, with a "customer" called W.W. Smith, actually a dummy company to expand profits for himself and confederates. Price Waterhouse (now PricewaterhouseCoopers) was Girard's auditor and, using only documents provided by Musica, never discovered the fraud.

With Girard reporting large profits and growth, Musica was able to acquire MR. Fraud expanded, while Price continued as auditor and continued to give unqualified (clean) opinions. With excellent audited financial statements, MR was a blue chip borrower and issued more stock and debt. MR developed a national distribution chain for pharmaceuticals, which did not exist before Musica, considerably expanding growth, profits, and debt. Simultaneously, dummy companies and fraud expanded as well. Most American subsidiaries were legitimate but a Canadian subsidiary was a dummy corporation. Bogus documents showed fraudulent sales, inventory, and receivables, claiming substantial profits and assets of $20 million—about 23% of MR's total assets.

The fraud was discovered by an inside whistleblower, not Price Water-house. Julian Thompson, MR Treasurer, discovered both the bogus Canadian subsidiary and fake customer W.W. Smith. Thompson confronted Musica. Musica panicked and put MR into bankruptcy. The SEC and the New York Attorney General investigated. Musica was arrested and after receiving bail, killed himself. Most confederates pled guilty, became government witnesses, and avoided jail. Only Controller John McGloon was actually sent to prison. MR was reorganized and emerged from bankruptcy in 1941. The SEC report claimed: "the financial statements [audited] by Price Waterhouse & Co. [were] materially false and misleading."

An embarrassed accounting profession conducted an AIA investigation uncovering major audit deficiencies. This led to a new AIA committee to establish formal auditing standards, later called generally accepted auditing standards (GAAS).[9] McKesson Corporation still exists and is part of the S&P 500. Ironically, McKesson was involved in another accounting scandal 60 years later, when it acquired medical information system firm HBO & Company (HBOC) and accounting irregularities were later discovered.

Auditing and Audit Reform

The concept of auditing started in the Middle Ages, reviewing reports orally (from the Latin *audire*). The relationship of auditors and business started in the 18th century, but the development of "professional accountants" performing audits by reviewing the books of business and relevant documents really started in 19th-century Great Britain (11 people were listed as accountants in 1799, growing to 1,000 by 1900). Professional organization began in Britain in that century: the Institute of Accountants in Edinburgh (1853) and the Institute of Chartered Accountants of England and Wales (1880). A number of what became the Big Eight accounting firms were established in mid-19th-century Britain, including Price, Waterhouse, Coopers, Peat, Deloitte, and Whinney.

Several British accountants, often sponsored by their firms, immigrated and practiced in America. The predecessor body to the AIA was founded in 1887 (the name was changed to AIA in 1917 and AICPA in 1957). New York became the first state to license CPAs, followed by Pennsylvania and Maryland. All states licensed CPAs by the early 1920s. In the United States, little regulation beyond licensing existed. Few rules were written and the scope of the audit (what was actually covered by the audit) was determined by the client. The AIA created the first code of ethics in 1917; many provisions protected the firms from competition such as bans on advertising and client solicitation.

Despite the lack of standardization, the "balance sheet" audit developed to check all transactions and balance sheet accounts and trace all vouchers, receipts, and other documents through the accounting records. Banks first used audits as a method to ensure the accuracy of financial statements and the ability to pay back loans, followed by investors evaluating earnings and dividend potential. Bankers and the public typically believed audits would uncover fraud, although auditors seldom made that claim.

In this era before regulation, considerable abuse was common. A corporate prospectus or annual report might list an audit but not include the report. The user would have no idea of the scope or outcome of the audit. The auditor might withdraw from an audit due to discovered (and uncorrected) abuses, but the outside user would not find out. The Federal Reserve and FTC published "Uniform Accounts" in the *Federal Reserve Bulletin* (which included audit methods used by Price Waterhouse), to be used as a standard audit practice, but compliance was voluntary (and not widespread). On the other hand, 90% of NYSE firms were audited by 1926.

The AIA established the Committee on Auditing Procedure (CAuP) in 1939 to consider audit deficiencies in light of MR. The first pronouncement, called Statement on Auditing Procedure (SAP) No. 1, specifically mandated observing inventory and confirming receivables, the practices missing in the MR audit. It also included other requirements, such as selecting the auditor either by the stockholders or the board of directors and an auditor's report that included an evaluation of internal controls. The SEC (ASR 21) mandated the auditors to state in the report whether the audit followed "GAAS," that is, those prescribed by the CAuP. The CAuP continued issuing SAPs (54) until replaced by another committee, called the Auditing Standards Executive Committee. This process of the profession-mandated audit standards continued until the Sarbanes-Oxley Act of 2002 created the semi-public Public Companies Accounting Oversight Board (PCAOB—it is technically a nonprofit organization rather than a government agency) to establish audit standards and regulate the audits of public companies.

Lessons to be Learned

The early 20th century saw substantial federal regulatory responses to economic catastrophes, especially FDR's New Deal after the Great Depression. This period established the basic mechanisms of financial reporting, as well as accounting and audit standard setting. This level of regulation, along with strict enforcement and rule changes as needed (such as audit standard requirements after the discovery of fraud at MR), worked reasonably well, especially over the next quarter century. Thus, the potential for effective regulation was demonstrated.

CHAPTER 4

War and Post–World War II Business and Corruption

Then came the 1970s. The old aversion to lawsuits fell by the wayside. It became easier to borrow money. Federal regulations were relaxed. Markets became internationalized. Investors became more aggressive, and the result was a boom in the number and size of corporate takeovers.

—Malcolm Gladwell

World War II business was about the war effort and avoiding war profiteering. Senator Harry Truman led a special senate committee on the national defense program (Truman Committee), propelling him to the vice presidency and the White House. As with all wars, war profiteering was, in fact, rampant. It was estimated that Truman Committee findings saved the country $10–15 billion, when a billion dollars was real money. After the war, with Europe and Asia in ruins, the United States was the economic colossus with half the world's production.

The "American model" of manufacturing perfected at General Motors had the management and accounting techniques to emulate. In many ways economic conditions were near-perfect, with high economic growth supported by strong exports, low unemployment, low inflation, educational opportunities, and a rising middle class. Lows included frequent recessions, issues with racism, women's rights, pollution, and unsustainable political promises. For a variety of reasons, imports would start outstripping exports. Deficiencies in the American model appeared, including inflation as an increasing problem. Investment banking was relatively small with limited power after World War II, but began to flex its growing muscles in the post-war period. So-called financial innovations over the next quarter century included hostile takeovers, leveraged buyouts, junk bonds, and increasing use of derivatives and structured finance.

Fraud did not disappear, but was held in check, usually big fraud at small companies or small fraud at big companies. Over the post–World War II period, the magnitude of fraud and other illicit acts continued to grow, because of increasing opportunities, rising power by banks, and the "innovations" that would be taken to extremes for mergers, market manipulation, and global bribery. The Securities Acts became less effective as banking and industrial power increased and the Securities and Exchange Commission (SEC) budget fell. The argument: regulation stifles innovation; however, innovation can mean great economic advances or greater opportunities to manipulate and cheat the system.

Business in War and Peace

The attack on Pearl Harbor in late 1941 brought war to an unprepared country. Military setbacks continued well into 1942. It took some time for industry to move from a consumer focus to war footing. Factories produced prodigious amounts of war materials, requiring massive spending, high taxes, and gigantic borrowing. One of the lasting policy innovations was income tax withholding in 1943. Workers paid taxes through withholding from each paycheck, producing higher taxes and fewer complaints over the previous annual lump-sum payment. Big government and high taxes continued after the war.

Connections between the military and business have been around at least since the Revolution, with inflated prices, bribery, extortion, and influence peddling common place. Union contracts were extremely valuable during the Civil War, where spending reached billions of dollars. Abraham Lincoln called the profiteers "worse than traitors." During World War I the government created the War Industrial Board to acquire munitions efficiently and reduce fraud and waste. Du Pont, originally a gun powder manufacturer, was a major beneficiary of government contracts. Du Pont became a major, diversified predominately chemical company funded by the massive profits from World War I contracts—Du Pont charged much higher rates to European allies than to the American military, apparently an acceptable form of war profiteering.

Franklin Roosevelt railed about the profiteering of "war millionaires" during World War II. The Senate Special Committee to Investigate the

National Defense Program, chaired by Harry S. Truman, held hearings and investigated war plants across the country. The focus was on inefficiency, waste, and war profiteering. Truman started at Fort Leonard Wood in his home state of Missouri, where construction was reputed to be wasteful and overpriced; military contractors seemed unaccountable, producing poor quality products at inflated prices. In addition to hearings and personal inspections by committee staff, the committee relied on whistleblowers. The Truman Committee saved the country billions and monitored defective output. An excess-profits tax was raised to 90% in an attempt to eliminate abuses.

President Dwight D. Eisenhower in his 1961 farewell address stated: "In the councils of government, we must guard against the acquisition of unwarranted influence, whether sought or unsought, by the military-industrial complex." Retired military often work for defense contractors, a reciprocal relationship not necessarily in the best interests of public policy. The basic concept can be extended to all forms of reciprocal relationships between business and government involving spending, special interest influence, and other forms of legal corruption. Public policy issues are complex, dynamic, and subject to abuse. Part of the analysis of business corruption is the abuse of the political process.

With much of Europe and Asia destroyed, the end of World War II brought economic dominance to the United States, with pundits describing it as the American Century. General Motors was the model for efficient big industrial business, commanding half of the domestic automobile market; American producers controlled 99% of the domestic American auto market and exported cars overseas. The chief executive officer (CEO) of GM, Charles ("Engine Charlie") Wilson, stated: "What was good for the country was good for General Motors, and vice versa." America continued to dominate, but foreign countries became increasingly competitive. Rising imports and trade deficits, recessions, labor problems, government budget deficits, and inflation became increasingly problematic. By the 1970s and 1980s, General Motors was no longer the model for industrial efficiency or high-quality products.

Conglomerates became the bustling new business model in the second half of the 20th century, thanks in part to accounting gimmicks. The era had its share of corporate fraud and bribery, especially of foreign officials.

Banking became a dynamic money machine beginning in the 1980s, powered by math wizards (quants) generating "financial innovations" using high-risk bets and lots of borrowed money. A gigantic insider trading, junk bond, and savings and loan conspiracy centered on junk bond king Michael Milken in the 1980s. Additional scandals occurred throughout the 1990s, as the tech boom led to fabulous new products and a euphoric investing public.

Merger Accounting and Manipulation

A merger combines two companies into one corporate entity, a common practice since the Civil War as corporations eliminated "excessive competition" and attempted to create monopoly power. These were horizontal mergers involving direct competitors. Vertical mergers were those in related industries. Andrew Carnegie's steel company, for example, acquired iron ore, coal, and transportation companies to ensure continued supply of basic materials and to lower costs. This strategy of acquiring business components from raw materials to transportation and distribution became a common business approach for big business—and part of a long process of the development of professional management. The third category was conglomerate mergers, the acquisition of a completely unrelated business. General Electric is an example of a 19th-century corporation becoming a successful global conglomerate, with operations from aircraft engines to finance (and, before discontinuing these operations, light bulbs and National Broadcasting Company).

Cleverly Rigged Accounting Ploys (CRAP)

Two theories of acquisition accounting developed and were standardized in the 1960s by the Accounting Principles Board. The first was pooling of interests, which presumed the combining of "equal" companies using historical cost. The resulting company would record the assets and liabilities of the two companies based on existing book values without regard to current values. Depreciated property, plant, and equipment could have a relatively low book value and be a fraction of current (replacement) cost. Patents and other intangible assets stayed unrecorded.

Inventory could be manipulated down, for example, due to perceived obsolete inventory or expected bad debts. In total, the result could be a low asset base and lower future operating expenses. The second theory, the purchase method, assumed that one company (the parent) acquired another (the subsidiary) and the accounting comes closer to economic reality. Using actual acquisition price (based on a cash or stock purchase) resulted in assets and liability restated to "fair value" (usually upward, sometimes by a lot), including the value of patents and other intangible assets. Of course, fair value is determined by "professional judgment." The difference between the acquisition price and restated fair value of net assets (the "premium paid") resulted in goodwill, something of a plug figure, for this difference.

Abe Brillof, Distinguished Professor Emeritus at Baruch College, used the term CRAP to describe "dirty pooling." His point was acquisition accounting could be used to generate manipulated profits using accounting practices allowable at the time. Acquisition assets could be recorded at historic cost or some measure of fair value based on "judgment." Assets that would be sold quickly could be recorded at a low value to generate a substantial gain on sale. Depreciable assets could be recorded at a high value to minimize taxes. Using dirty pooling some assets could be valued based on pooling while others were based on the purchase method. Accounting standards on acquisitions changed to eliminate the most blatant abuse, although acquiring firms still have considerable flexibility in valuations—now based exclusively on the purchase method.

Conglomerates

One long-time business strategy is the acquisition of diverse companies and this became a speculative obsession in the 1950s. The managers claimed that the industry was irrelevant when competent management was introduced: a "highly efficient" parent could turn around a floundering subsidiary by cutting unnecessary costs and improving operating efficiency. The other argument was diversity—with subsidiaries in many industries the conglomerate could thrive even during recession. Major conglomerates of the time such as Textron or Ling-Temco-Vaught (LTV)

achieved big premiums (high price/earnings ratios), making stock acquisitions of low premium subsidiaries seemingly a bargain. The "great management" argument was oversold, but the key strategy for profitability
was acquisition accounting, using dirty pooling and other forms of CRAP.
(Note that continued growth, and merger manipulation could work for
any acquisitive firms, not just conglomerates.)

This scheme worked for decades. Continued low-priced acquisitions
fueled growth—the company was bigger, with more revenues and income,
whether well run or not. Accounting gimmicks could make up for any
management shortcomings. James Ling started with an electrical contract
business and then went on a buying binge in the 1950s: L.M. Electronics
in 1956, Temco Aircraft and Chance Vaught Aerospace, forming LTV.
LTV became an industrial giant. According to Geisst[1] the Ling's strategy
was "Buy them, incorporate their earnings, and then sell part of them off
to a hungry investing public and use the proceeds to buy something else."
Ling relied on credit to finance his empire. When profits dropped in the
late 1960s, Ling was fired. LTV survived only by selling off subsidiaries
and avoided bankruptcy until 2000.

International Telephone and Telegraph (ITT) also started in the
1950s. Founder Harold Geneen acquired some 350 companies. An antitrust investigation discovered that ITT overstated earnings by 70% using
merger manipulations and the Justice Department brought suit. Political
payoffs by Geneen were used to stay in business, including $400,000
to the reelection campaign of Richard Nixon and a $1 million payment
to the Central Intelligence Agency to protect ITT's interests in Chile.
Conglomerates Litton and Gulf + Western used political payoffs to promote defense contracts.

The success could not last. With operating problems in difficult
industries, recessions, inflation, dollar devaluations overseas, and big debt
payments, profits cratered. As the price premiums declined and leverage
became too high, further acquisitions were no longer possible. Leaders
were fired and conglomerates were no longer fashionable. The last major
conglomerate scandal was Tyco in the early 21st century. On the other
hand, conglomerates can work. General Electric continues to be a successful conglomerate, as do reorganized firms Textron and ITT.

Hostile Takeovers, Leveraged Buyouts (LBOs), Junk Bonds, and the Destruction of an Industry

Merger strategies took additional ugly turns during the last quarter of the 20th century. More acquisitions were hostile takeovers, which meant acquiring the companies without the permission of the board of directors. Insiders and well-financed outsiders took over companies using LBOs, borrowing to finance the takeover. Much of this debt was in the form of junk bonds (risky, noninvestment grade bonds). Michael Milken created a junk bond empire at investment bank Drexel Burnham, using underhanded methods that including insider trading, deceptively investing in accounts of family members and confederates for personal gain, manipulating junk bond prices, and enticing the newly deregulated savings and loans (S&Ls) to invest in his high-risk offerings. If all of these are considered simultaneously, this could be considered the largest business scandal in American history.

Hostile Takeovers

Big business and investment banking divisions specializing in mergers and acquisitions look to find corporate targets based on bargain prices, market share benefits, specialized expertise, or other potentially positive factors. Almost always, the potential buyer sends out feelers to the CEO and board of directors of the target firm. The board of the target can accept the offer or ask for a higher price—part of the "friendly takeover" process. If friendly, the buyer usually can access the records of the target for a thorough due diligence review. The target has other alternatives: reject the offer out of hand or seek another buyer, a "white knight."

Generally, "until the 1970s, it was considered scandalous for one company to buy another company without the target agreeing to be bought. ... Then came the 1970s. The old aversion to lawsuits fell by the wayside. It became easier to borrow money. Federal regulations were relaxed. Investors became more aggressive, and the result was a boom in the number and size of corporate takeovers."[2] The first hostile takeover was the American firm Reynolds Metals attempting to acquire British Aluminum in the late 1950s, successful although British Aluminum fought the takeover and sought a white knight. During the 1960s, Northwest Industrial was stopped by potential target B.F. Goodrich, when Goodrich convinced the state of Ohio to block the merger.

The bidder going into hostile takeover mode uses expensive law firms and investment banks that specialize in hostile strategies. Alternative one is a proxy fight, seeking enough stockholders to replace current board members with bidder-friendly alternatives. The bidder can accumulate at least half the outstanding shares in a tender offer (the winner was determined in the "snake pit," the counting room where inspectors could be influenced by competing lawyers). In a "creeping tender," the bidder can buy target shares to accumulate enough shares to change the board. The bidder can use the media to accuse the target of incompetent management and operating blunders, while claiming to "rescue stockholders" with a large price premium—perhaps 25%–50% above the market price.

New York law firm Skadden, Arps became a hostile takeover specialist, initially hired by investment bank Morgan Stanley. Morgan Stanley's first takeover attempt involved International Nickel's (Inco) 1974 raid on Philadelphia battery maker Electric Storage Battery (ESB). ESB fought back, assisted by Goldman Sachs, finding a white knight in United Aircraft (now United Technologies). After a nasty bidding war, Inco won but at a cost of $41 a share—the original offer was $27. After Morgan, several other banks pushed hostile takeovers, while Goldman and others specialized in hostile takeover defenses.

The 1970s produced economic conditions favorable to the acquirers, with high inflation and a long-term bear market with stock prices down substantially. It became more inexpensive to acquire a rival or complementary firm than starting from scratch and expanding internally. With mergers left and right, virtually all corporations except the giants felt threatened. Competent companies with less debt, substantial liquidity, and steady earnings were prime targets. The solution seemed to be to become less compelling: increase debt, reduce cash, and insert poison pills (provisions to make the company less attractive such as a huge payment to management in case of a hostile takeover). All in all, this did not make American business attractive or more productive.

The Reagan presidency of the 1980s proved business friendly, antitrust became almost a nonissue, and mergers increased. Junk bonds became more available, the number of acquisitions, hostile and friendly, increased as did the size of the targets. Blue chip companies got into the action. Du Pont acquired Conoco in 1981 for the astronomical (at the time) price of $7.8 billion after a bidding war with three other firms and almost double the original market value of Conoco. Michael Milken's empire reached its peak and helped facilitate both hostile takeovers and leveraged buyouts. Private equity companies, often using hostile takeovers, got bigger and more powerful at this time.[3]

Leveraged Buyouts

The high-risk LBO became a speculator's and would-be-billionaire's dream. The target would be bought on borrowed money, usually using high-cost junk bonds with the target's assets serving as collateral. A ruthless entrepreneur could get in, sell off pieces of the acquisition, reorganize operations to cut costs (with massive layoffs and reduced salaries and benefits being a significant strategy), and use manipulative merger accounting to show increasing profitability. The acquisition by McLean Industries of Pan-Atlantic Shipping in the mid-1950s is usually given credit as the first LBO, with $42 million borrowed of the $49 million price tag (86%).

Milken created a vast high-priced junk bond market, by then populated with private equity firms created to specialize in takeovers. Various players were called venture capitalists (usually investing in startups) and vulture capitalists (usually taking over firms close to failure) and exhibited a wide range of ethical standards. Success meant billions in profits; failure meant bankruptcy for the target and possibly the private equity fund. Equity firms (and major junk bond users), such as Kohlberg, Kravis, and Roberts (KKR), T. Boone Pickens, Victor Posner, and James Goldsmith, became major LBO players. KKR bought RJR Nabisco in 1989 for $31 billion after a bidding war increased the share price from $75 to $109, the largest LBO of the time. Milken's empire and the junk bond market would collapse at the end of the 1980s, but both LBO and junk bonds would be resurrected and even more common in the 1990s and

21st century. Twenty-first century LBOs included Toys "R" Us, Metro-Goldwyn-Mayer, Chrysler, Hertz, and Hospital Corporation of America.

Michael Milken's Junk Bond Empire

Bond ratings have been around since financial analyst John Moody used letter grades to assess credit risk beginning in 1909. Moody's ratings start at Aaa for the highest quality bonds, down to C for really risky bonds. Those between Baa and Aaa were considered "investment grade," satisfactory for conservative investing. Below Baa were the speculative bonds, affectionately known as junk bonds. To better appeal to investors, these were called "high income" bonds. Early on, virtually all bonds seeking a bond rating achieved an investment grade rating; without it, the bonds could not be easily issued through investment banks—better to stay unrated that be called speculative. Junk bonds were mainly "fallen angels," those initially rated investment grade but fallen on hard times and downgraded. Milken would change that.

Milken started as a bond researcher and trader at the firm that became Drexel, Burnham and Lambert, at a time when investment banks traded almost exclusively with investment grade bonds. Milken was familiar with research showing that a diversified portfolio of junk bonds provided a higher total risk-adjusted return than investment grade bonds. He started a junk bond trading group at Drexel in the 1970s set up in Southern California. S&Ls became major investors when the industry was deregulated in the early 1980s. With little competition, Milken dominated this growing market, especially setting prices. This was basically an unregulated market with little public information. Milken controlled junk bond prices to maintain huge spreads and massive profits for Drexel and himself.

A significant new market was the creation of primary junk bond issues, starting with a $30 million Texas Instruments issue in the 1970s. Milken's customer base bought the TI bonds and other new issues followed. Default rates stayed low, thanks to Milken. When companies had difficulty making interest and principal payments, the bonds were restructured and new issues floated. His empire was a perfect fit for the hostile takeover/LBO markets of the time. Private equity traders became Milken clients, using junk bonds to go after much of American business: Boone

Pickens went after Unocal, Victor Posner got Sharon Steel in a hostile takeover, and James Goldsmith went after Crown Zellerbach. KKR's takeover of Beatrice Foods, Storer Communications, and RJR Nabisco were financed in part through Milken's junk bonds.

Although he had a gigantic compensation package at Drexel, he set up private agreements and partnerships to further enrich himself, family, and friends using insider information—violating both Drexel policy and the law. Arbitrageur Ivan Boesky was a Milken co-conspirator, using information supplied by Milken and various investment bankers. Boesky, for example, would make big bets following Milken's orders and the two would later split the profits. According to Stewart,[4] "Milken and Boesky were deeply intertwined in what was a sweeping criminal conspiracy. Taken together, the ventures were practically a catalogue of securities crimes, starting with insider trading, and including false public disclosures, tax fraud, and market manipulation, as well as a slew of more technical crimes. … The crimes were mere way stations toward outcomes, such as hostile takeovers, that were, on their face, perfectly legal."

At the end of the 1980s, with the S&L industry in shambles and many industries in trouble, Milken's clients failed in large numbers, about 25% of Drexel-financed firms, and the junk boom collapsed. Milken and Drexel were indicted under the Racketeer Influence and Corrupt Organizations Act. Drexel declared bankruptcy after pleading guilty. Milken pled guilty to securities fraud, insider trading, and other felonies, sentenced to 10 years in prison and fined over $1 billion.

S&L Debacle

S&Ls were designed to take in short-term deposits and make long-term mortgages, which worked as long as interest rates were low and stable. That changed in the 1970s as high inflation forced interest rates to rise. S&Ls had to raise interest rates to maintain their deposit base, but were still stuck with low-interest mortgages. In a misguided attempt to avert the total collapse of the industry, Congress passed the Garn-St. Germain Act in 1982 deregulating the industry. The S&Ls could do all sorts of investing and other activities—areas they knew nothing about. A single individual could now own an S&L (the old rule was a minimum 400 investors), allowing building contractors, organized crime, and assorted others to buy S&Ls with every intent of manipulating the system.

With few regulatory constraints, the industry exploded to $1.5 trillion in assets. A major source of funding was high-priced jumbo certificates of deposit, while high-yielding junk bonds became a major investment category—Milken was the early supplier of the industry. Corrupt executives introduced a multitude of illicit practices, from speculation to self-serving activities in commercial real estate including fraud. Perhaps the most corrupt executive was Charles Keating of Lincoln Savings headquartered in Phoenix, Arizona. Keating was a major investor in junk bonds and relied on accounting fraud to maintain his empire. This included property swaps with other companies to claim profits on sales. A regulatory audit discovered much of the abuse, including unreported losses of $135 million. Lincoln was seized by the government and Keating indicted. He pled guilty to fraud and sentenced to 12 years in jail.

The collapse of the industry required a federal bailout and Congress established the Resolution Trust Corporation (RTC) to dispose of the real estate of over 700 failed S&Ls. The estimated cost was $250 billion, although the final net cost to the federal government was $87 billion. The RTC was disbanded in 1995, after the liquidation was completed.

Small Companies, Big Fraud

From the end of World War II roughly to the 1970s was an era of low inflation and low volatility in securities markets plus the general view that little corruption existed. The securities laws seemed to be working, including improving accounting and auditing standards. Wall Street was relatively "un-manipulative" with little obvious speculation; regulatory agencies were viewed as diligent and tough. The major accounting firms, the "Big Eight" (at the time made up of Arthur Andersen, Coopers & Lybrand, Haskins & Sells, Ernst & Ernst, Peat, Marwick Mitchell, Price Waterhouse, Touche Ross, and Arthur Young) were considered elite, hard-working, and competent. Despite this overall view of relative harmony, corporate fraud cases erupted periodically challenging the overall view of auditors. Among the most infamous were Investors Overseas Services (IOS), Equity Funding, National Student Marketing, EMS

Governmental Securities, and ZZZZ Best, mainly big frauds at small companies. These were hits to investor confidence rather than economic chaos. Later fraud cases into the 1990s included bigger companies, such as Waste Management, Sunbeam, and Cendant.

Recurring frauds demonstrate several important points. First, the potential for corruption and fraud is always present, driven by incentives to cheat by ethically challenged individuals and corporate cultures. Consequently, the need for internal controls, diligent reviews, and audits, plus aggressive regulators remains constant. Auditors are not incredibly good at detecting fraud—the auditors claim this is not their job; the public, on the other hand, thinks it is. This created what was called the "expectations gap." It turns out that whistle-blowers have always been the most common detectors of fraud, not auditors or regulators. A related problem is that auditors are hired and paid by the corporate clients. The auditors' incentives include being as accommodative as possible to the client—rejecting every controversial practice normally does not result in long-term relationships with corporate clients. Audit staff and managers point out and document accounting and reporting "gray areas," and it is up to the managing partner to reach consensus with the chief financial officer (CFO) and audit committee on what is acceptable for the audit firm to issue an unqualified (clean) opinion.

The individual cases have unique circumstances that require review, including the incentives and character of the individuals involved, the overall business environment and culture, and the economic and regulatory framework at the time. The small company-big fraud cases of the early postwar period can be considered "outliers," not typical of most corporations. The 1990s frauds involved larger companies, widespread fraud, and more likely represented a common corporate culture of manipulation and aggressive accounting in a period of lax enforcement.[5]

Investors Overseas Services

IOS was a Swiss mutual fund, run by crooked Americans—one of the rare cases when one fraudster was replaced by another fraudster. New Yorker Bernard Cornfeld founded the company in 1955 to sell mutual funds mainly to the American military stressing tax avoidance and lax regulations. IOS grew to $2.5 billion in assets. The SEC forced IOS to shut down American operations in 1965, accusing the company of securities violations. The company collapsed at the end of the 1960s, and Cornfeld was fired. He was charged with fraud by the Swiss regulators but acquitted after spending almost a year in jail.

Robert Vesco was the CEO of conglomerate International Controls Corp and bought IOS in 1970 using a LBO, turning it into a holding company with offices in remote locations to avoid regulators. Vesco proceeded to loot the company, using dummy companies to move some $235 million to other remote locations. The SEC investigated and charged Vesco with embezzlement. He fled to Costa Rica and spent the rest of his life on the run, becoming the "undisputed king of the fugitive financiers."[6] Vesco became especially infamous by contributing vast sums to Richard Nixon. Congressional hearings followed in the 1970s, but did not result in new regulations.

ZZZZ Best

Barry Minkow founded ZZZZ Best (pronounced "Zee Best") when still in high school. It was an insurance restoration company, starting as a carpet cleaning service in the 1980s. Thanks to fraud (such things as check kiting and false credit card charges), stealing, and a crooked CFO in Charles Arrington, Minkow got bank loans based on bogus financial statements. The company was audited, but the auditors relied on fake documents reporting substantial revenues from insurance companies and false examples of restoration projects in progress.

Minkow's company went public in 1986, listed on NASDAQ (an American stock exchange competing with the NYSE). From the initial public offering of $15 million, the stock price rose to $18 a share in 1987, giving the company a market value of $100 million. Minkow also used Milken's junk bonds to acquire a larger carpet cleaning company, KeyServe. Like many other frauds, Minkow became too successful to hide his inglorious past. *The Los Angeles Times* reported Minkow's fake credit card use, and then accounting firm Ernst and Whinney resigned from the audit after discovering fraud. The internal investigation by ZZZZ Best discovered embezzlement by Minkow of over $20 million, forcing him to resign. Indictments and convictions were not far behind and in 1989 Minkow was sentenced to 25 years in prison for securities fraud, racketeering, and embezzlement. He served seven years and then after his release was convicted of insider trading in another company.

Other Scandals in 1960s to 1980s

Allied Crude Vegetable Oil borrowed money based on its inventory of salad oil. Company CEO Tino De Angelis had ships filled with water and salad oil on top; inspectors confirmed the oil inventory. The fraud was discovered in 1963—De Angelis spent seven years in jail. American Express was the biggest loser, writing off $58 million in the "Great Salad Oil Swindle."

Continental Vending became a successful criminal case brought against the auditor, Lybrand, Ross Brothers & Montgomery (now part of PricewaterhouseCoopers, a Big Four auditor), for certifying financial statements the auditor knew were false. A subsidiary of Continental Vending Machine Corp. borrowed a large sum from the parent for the benefit of an executive unable to repay a loan. The loan was still recorded as an asset on the books of Continental. Although Lybrand claimed Continental was correctly following generally accepted auditing standards, three Lybrand auditors were found guilty of criminal fraud in 1969.

National Student Marketing was established by Cortes Randell in 1964 to provide jobs to college students and other services. Randell claimed this was a $100 million conglomerate, with tremendous growth in earnings and assets. He cashed out before the authorities discovered the company was bogus. That did not get him off the hook and he was convicted of stock fraud and spent a year and a half in prison.

Founded in 1964, Equity Funding Corporation of America sold life insurance; the innovation was the use of policy cash values to buy mutual funds. When expected profits did not materialize, the financial reports were falsified. To generate cash, the policies were sold to other insurance companies (reinsurance). To actually pay back the reinsurers, bogus policies were created, along with all the necessary documentation to maintain the insurance year after year. Killing off imaginary customers on policies shipped to the reinsurers generated additional cash (there were no relatives to receive the proceeds). Whistle-blowers tipped off the California regulators. Equity Funding was shut down in 1972 as the SEC was investigating. Several Equity Funding executives were convicted of fraud and sent to jail.

In a strange twist of the Equity Funding case, whistle-blower Ray Dirks was charged with insider trading by the SEC and the case went to the Supreme Court before Dirks was acquitted. This was a period when neither insider trading nor whistle-blowing was well defined. Despite additional regulations and court cases, both whistle-blowing and insider trading are still problematic.

The Baptist Foundation of Arizona was founded in the 1940s to support Baptist causes. The Foundation lost its way by the 1990s under a new management, losing over $3 million in 1992 from "dubious transactions." Instead of coming clean, the organization hid the losses, started even more illicit transactions, and siphoned off cash to Foundation executives and board members. These included borrowing heavily, an investment Ponzi scheme to bring in more cash, land-flipping, and other bogus real estate deals. The Foundation went bankrupt in 1999, with over $500 million in liabilities and only $70 million in assets. Several executives and directors were eventually convicted of fraud and sent to prison. Arthur Andersen was the auditor and settled by agreeing to pay over $200 million to bilked investors.

Waste Management

Waste Management was a 1968 merger of two garbage collection business owned by Dean Buntrock and Wayne Huizenga. Buntrock took control in the 1980s after Huizenga stepped down and later founded Blockbuster. Business boomed, particularly as local governments privatized garbage and Waste Management stepped in—acquiring some 100 garbage and landfill enterprises. Waste Management used a combination strategy of lobbying, political contributions, and, when necessary, outright bribes. The company developed a reputation for violating environmental rules and antitrust laws, resulting in substantial fines.

On top of these lapses, Waste Management increasingly used earnings manipulation and blatant fraud to meet analysts' expectations as this industry got more competitive and less profitable. By the 1990s, the company was manipulating merger and fixed asset accounting. Expenses could be understated by increasing the salvage value of property and making the useful lives of plant and equipment longer. Operating costs of landfills also were capitalized. The most blatant form of fraud was recording gains on sham transactions.

A familiar name in allowing aggressive accounting, Arthur Andersen was the auditor. Andersen apparently was well aware of many if not most of the tricks, but continued to give Waste Management a clean opinion by claiming the transactions were immaterial. The SEC investigated and charged "defendants' improper accounting practices were centralized at corporate headquarters. ... They monitored the company's actual operating results and compared them to the quarterly targets set in the budget."[7] Waste Management understated expenses by $1.7 billion and the SEC forced the company to restate earnings for fiscal years 1992 through 1997—the largest restatement up to that time. Both Waste Management and Andersen were fined by the SEC and forced to settle stockholder lawsuits. The company was acquired by USA Waste Services, which kept the Waste Management name. That was not the end; new fraud was discovered and an additional $1.2 billion had to be written off. Despite the abuse, Waste Management is still around with a market value of $17 billion.

Cendant

Cendant was the result of the acquisition of CUC (Comp-U-Card) International by Hospitality Franchise Systems (HFS) in 1997 and a name change. HFS owned hotel franchises, including Howard Johnson, Ramada, and Days Inn, with much of the growth from acquisitions. Unfortunately for HFS stockholders, CUC had been committing fraud for years. CUC had a membership-for-a-fee program to sell consumer products with extended payments. CUC CEO Walter Forbes used the common strategy when failing to meet analyst expectations—manipulate, a strategy started in the early 1980s. Merger manipulation led the list, the ability to determine valuations of acquisitions, use merger reserve accounts, and so on. Advertising costs and various operating expenses were capitalized, write-offs were ignored, while revenues were recognized aggressively (including immediate recognition on long-term sales, which should have been deferred). Other revenue accounts were bogus. In other words, a long list of items were manipulated and fraudulently reported quarterly over a long period.

CUC ran out of manipulation tricks by 1996 as real losses were growing and hiding fraud became increasingly difficult. HFS, before the acquisition, discovered no fraud at CUC and completed the $14 billion merger. Fraud was discovered in 1998, only months after the merger was completed. Restatement of earlier years was required, reducing Cendant's income by $440 million. Indictments against the former CUC executives and investor lawsuits against Cendant and auditor Ernst & Young followed. The settlements with investors totaled $3 billion, a record up to that time. Walter Forbes, the former CUC CEO, was convicted and sentenced to 12 years in prison plus substantial fines. Cendant recovered but later split into several companies—none of which used the Cendant name.

Sunbeam

Sunbeam was a consumer products manufacturing company, created in 1989 from the ashes of bankrupt company Allegheny International. It manufactured products under the Sunbeam name and several others, including Coleman, Mr. Coffee, and Oster. When performance declined in the early 1990s, the board of directors hired outsider Albert Dunlap to restructure the company in 1996. Dunlap had a track record as a turnaround specialist at Scott Paper, where stock prices increased over 200% while he was in charge. Dunlap's restructuring involved severe cost cutting and employee layoffs (some 11,000 at Scott Paper—earning his epithet "Chainsaw Al").

Living up to his nickname, Dunlap fired about half of Sunbeam's employees and wrote off $340 million in special charges. The special charges proved a form of accounting manipulation: the write-offs were blamed on the previous management and simultaneously created reserve accounts for future write-offs (called "cookie jar reserve") to make the performance under his watch look better. It was just the start of manipulation and fraud. Aggressive revenue recognition included "channel stuffing" and "bill-and-hold sales" (pushing out inventory to customers by promising huge discounts and recording revenues before actual sales, respectively). On the expense side, a multitude of tactics were used. Operating expenses were capitalized or just not recorded, such as warranty costs, sales returns, and advertising. Other costs were charged directly to restructuring; that is, using those cookie jar reserves. The market loved it. Stock price rose from 12.50 when he started, peaking at 52, up over 400%.

When manipulation was not enough to meet analysts' forecasts, Dunlap turned to outright fraud, recording bogus sales as revenue. Auditor Arthur Andersen understood the manipulation, but gave Sunbeam an unqualified opinion anyway in 1997. Despite the accommodating auditor, Sunbeam still missed analyst forecasts for the year. It was only after the press made negative statements about Sunbeam that the board of directors started an internal investigation. They discovered the manipulation and fraud, firing both Dunlap and the CFO. Earnings were restated in 1998. The SEC later claimed that Sunbeam "created the illusion of a successful restructuring to inflate its stock price and thus improve its value as an acquisition target."[8] Investor lawsuits of Sunbeam and Andersen followed. Sunbeam went bankrupt in 2001, only to restructure and emerge as American Household in 2002. American Household was acquired by Jarden Corp. in 2004.

Financial Fraud Gets Complex and Goes Global

As Japan, Europe, and various developing countries were growing their economies in the post–World War II period, American companies, capital, and expertise followed. Global opportunities attracted financial "innovators" and speculators, and various speculative excesses bubbled up. Derivative instruments (financial instruments derived from securities, others assets and related indices, including futures and options) became really significant after economists Fischer Black and Myron Scholes developed the famous Black-Scholes model in 1973 to price options (pricing models for everything derivative-related followed). Unfortunately, the respected derivatives in the hands of financial traders and quants were turned into complex instruments, leading to massive speculation hidden from the public and, ultimately, fiascoes. Part of the problem was that many of the buyers and sellers did not understand the instruments or the underlying costs and risks involved.

When the United States went off the gold standard in 1971, all currencies floated against one another, instead of being relatively fixed against the value placed on gold. Soon, foreign currency futures, swaps, and options became an essential financial activity. Some currencies would eventually collapse, often bringing down entire economies, made worse by potential speculation. Hedge fund manager George Soros helped bring down the British pound in 1992. Mexico's peso collapsed in 1995, followed by Thailand and a multitude of other Asian currencies. Russia followed. The Russian default would bring down the biggest of the hedge funds, Long-term Capital Management in 1998.

Continental Illinois became the first "too big to fail" bank, bailed out by the Federal Reserve in the mid-1980s. Investment bank Salomon Brothers almost went under due to a Treasury bond scandal in 1991 and was soon acquired by Travelers (now part of Citi Group). Derivatives broker Nicholas Leeson brought down the venerable British investment bank Barings in 1995, losing billions on unauthorized derivative trades using Tokyo's Nikkei futures.

A number of companies, governments, retirement funds, and insurance companies were sold risky, complex, and high-priced derivative-based investments by Wall Street, based on relative interest rates. The biggest victim was Orange County, California, which bought billions of toxic instruments and paid investment bank Merrill Lynch over $100 million in fees. Orange County Treasurer Robert Citron even borrowed additional billions to speculate on margin with these presumably "safe, high-yield investments." One of the most outrageous was the "inverse rate floaters," which paid a high interest rate—but minus London interbank interest rate (LIBOR) (LIBOR—see Timeline, 2012 for more on LIBOR manipulation). These and other instruments paid investors handsomely as long as short-term interest rates (in this case LIBOR) stayed low. But they did not. In the early 1990s, the Federal Reserve under Chairman Alan Greenspan increased rates and Orange County investments collapsed in 1994. The $1.8 billion loss resulted in the county's bankruptcy. Citron pled guilty to filing false statements, receiving probation. Orange County sued Merrill and eventually received $400 million to settle.

Other governments suffered losses, but nothing compared to Orange County. Many corporations had derivative losses around the same time, including Procter & Gamble (losing $100 million) and Gibson Greetings ($20 million). Investment banks developed a reputation of looking for easy targets ("dumb money," basically naïve investors) to sell expensive products to.

The bribery of foreign governments by American multinationals became a major scandal and resulted in a SEC investigation in the mid-1970s of over 400 major companies that admitted to bribing foreign governments (and related officials and political parties) plus additional potentially illegal acts. One of the most egregious examples was Lockheed's bribing officials of foreign governments to receive military contracts, including the Netherlands, West Germany, Italy, and Saudi Arabia. "Bananagate" focused on Latin American officials specifically for favorable terms on banana exports. A major difficulty was the widespread corruption in many foreign countries and the expectation of appropriate payoffs to receive favorable treatment. These issues led to additional regulations, including the Foreign Corrupt Practices Act, which banned bribery of foreign officials.

One of the most amazing stories was the Bank of Credit and Commerce International (BCCI) scandal, based on the rogue BCCI, founded in 1972 by Mohammed Zaigham Abbas, a Pakistani financier. The Sheikh of Abu Dhabi and Bank of America provided much of the initial funding, but Bank of America later withdrew most of its investments as evidence of fraud became apparent. BCCI grew to $20 billion in assets, with operations in almost 80 countries by the 1980s. BCCI was registered in Luxembourg, with operations run in Grand Cayman, Karachi, and London, a banking structure established to avoid regulatory restrictions. This required shell corporations and layers of opaque entities.

The results of BCCI operations included massive fraud, bribery, tax evasion, and money laundering to arms traffickers, drug dealers, and others. BCCI acquired U.S. banks secretly to avoid regulations designed to keep it out of the country and used well-known Americans for political influence. Investigations discovered the illegal activities and audits discovered millions of dollars that were lost. American indictments started in 1988 and regulators forced the worldwide liquidation of BCCI in the early 1990s. Robert Morgenthau, Manhattan District Attorney, called BCCI "the largest bank fraud in world financial history."

Regulatory Action

Federal, and to a lesser extent state and local, regulatory agencies were active throughout the period, usually involved in the discovery and prosecution of fraud and other illicit acts, but playing other roles as well. Sometimes the SEC and sundry federal agencies enforced the laws stringently and other times loosely. New laws were recommended and (occasionally) passed. Periods of strict enforcement existed, such as after the Foreign Corrupt Practices Act of 1977 following a number of major bribery cases. Periods of deregulation and/or slack enforcement happened during the Reagan administrations in the 1980s and around the time of the tech bubble in the late 1990s. It proved to be a bumpy ride for enforcement and economic activity in general.

Remove That Punch Bowl

Regulations and regulators generally were stringent early in the postwar period, a continuation of the substantial financial legislation of the Great Depression. Federal Reserve Chairman (from 1951 to 1970) William McChesney Martin famously stated: "The job of the Federal Reserve is to take away the punch bowl just as the party gets going." The 1950s were boom years, but suffered three minor recessions, largely because of Fed action to increase interest rates. Later Fed policy makers, like Nixon's Fed Chairman Arthur Burns, were more reluctant to take away that punch bowl—booms became longer, but so did the levels of manipulation and recessions.

As inflation increased in the later 1960s and 1970s, caused in part by federal budget deficits over wars in Vietnam and on poverty, President Nixon abandoned the gold standard (technically the gold reserve standard of the Bretton Woods Agreement, which established the foreign exchange system after World War II) in 1971. This made inflation worse, exacerbated by the massive oil price increases caused by the Organization of the Petroleum Exporting Countries. With stagflation rising (the combination of the unemployment rate and inflation rate, both over 10% around 1980) Fed Chairman Paul Volcker (1979–87) dramatically increased interest rate, which caused disruptions and recession, but tamed inflation by 1983.

President Reagan, first elected in 1980, preached deregulation and delivered. The economy boomed, as did manipulation and fraud. The S&L debacle previously described, showed the dark side of deregulation and lax enforcement (not only the collapse of an industry, but also massive insider trading and junk bond abuses)—and the direct cost to American taxpayers. Reagan appointed economist Alan Greenspan at Fed Chairman in 1987, a deregulation ideologue. Greenspan promoted economic growth and downplayed regulation, claiming that the market participants would regulate themselves. In fact, the extraordinary greed on Wall Street and in much of business America would be well displayed over the 20 years of Greenspan service. In addition, the Fed punch bowl would continue to be filled late into the proverbial party night.

A major example of Greenspan's blind spot to abuse and need for regulation was in derivative instruments, which boomed after the improved pricing models of the mid-1970s. Shortly after Greenspan became Fed chair, the Market Crash of 1987 resulted in the biggest one-day loss on the Dow Jones Industrial Average ever (23%). The major cause was the use of "portfolio insurance," a derivative play that tanked the market. Greenspan's Fed flooded the system with cash, limiting the damage. In the 1990s, massive derivative losses were suffered by governments (including Orange County), corporations, the collapse of Mexican, Asian, and Russian currencies, and the downfall of the biggest hedge fund, Long-term Capital Management. The Fed stepped in repeatedly to bail out Wall Street.

Given the massive abuse of derivatives literally worldwide, Brooksley Born, chairman of the Commodity Futures Trading Commission (CFTC), which regulates the formal futures and commodities markets, proposed modest regulation and CFTC oversight of over-the-counter (OTC) derivatives (the opaque derivatives that banks design for specific users and caused the 1990s problems). In Congressional hearings, Born was slapped down by Greenspan and officials at Treasury and the SEC. Instead, Congress passed the Commodities Futures Modernization Act of 2000, which called for the complete deregulation of OTC derivatives. Despite the many collapses involving derivatives and needed Fed bailouts, Greenspan won—the economy would soon pay the price.

Over an extended period, commercial and investment banks were growing and gathering political clout. Investment banks also were going public (traditionally, they were relatively conservative partnerships), taking on increasingly risky deals (they were now playing with other people's money) and paying massive compensation packages. Commercial and investment banks were also merging operations. Citibank led the way, merging with Travelers Insurance to form Citigroup in 1998 to create the biggest bank of the period. This violated the Depression-era Glass-Steagall Act and Citi lobbied to make the new mega-bank legal. Congress complied with the Gramm-Leach-Bliley Act (Financial Services Modernization Act of 1999). This allowed commercial and investment banks, as well as insurance firms and other financial operations, to consolidate. Too-big-to-fail became a significant issue. Basically, the early 21st century became a period of near-deregulation of Wall Street and banking. Congress and the regulators created a broken system and were slow to correct the mistakes.

Cycles of the Audit Risk Environment

Auditing thrived in the postwar period, with the Big Eight emerging as the premier accounting firms globally. Accounting and audit standards expanded and professionalism became increasingly important. CPA licensing requirements became more stringent, with many states requiring first a college degree and then instituting "five year programs" (terminology differed, but generally accounting students needed the equivalent of masters' degrees to become CPAs).

A major result of the widespread bribery and corruption of operating in foreign countries was the Foreign Corrupt Practices Act (FCPA) of 1977. The Act banned bribery of foreign officials—easier said than done when dealing with cultures of corruption. Other major countries later passed similar rules on bribery. Corporations have been prosecuted over suspected bribery ever since, such as McDonald's Mexican bribery scandal in 2012.

Of more importance to auditors was the FCPA requirement for adequate internal controls (procedures to ensure efficient and effective operations, reliable financial reporting, and legal compliance). If internal controls are reliable, the changes of fraud and certain types of manipulation are reduced. The Committee of Sponsoring Organizations (COSO) was created in 1985 to sponsor the National Commission on Fraudulent Financial Reporting (called the Treadway Commission after chairman James Treadway, a former commissioner of the SEC). This followed the multiple prosecutions of fraud and scandals of the period, earlier committees such as the 1974 Cohen Commission that discovered an "expectations gap" in what investors perceived were the auditor's responsibilities in detecting fraud, plus Congressional investigations and legislation—especially the FCPA. The Treadway Report issued in 1987 focused on fraud and emphasized the lack of proper internal control in major fraud cases. Based on the report, COSO studied internal control attempting to provide an overall framework. The framework described the process of effective operations, financial disclosure reliability, and complying with laws and regulation through risk assessment, monitoring, and other components.

While these regulatory attempts increased government oversight, other factors went in the opposite direction. In 1979 the Justice Department and Federal Trade Commission attempted to increase auditor competition and outlawed the profession's bans on competitive bidding and advertising. Competition increased, resulting in fierce bidding for new clients and the practice of "low balling," submitting a low bid to get the new client. As a result, profitability declined and many complained that it reduced "professional integrity."[9] The Private Securities Litigation Reform Act of 1995 limited auditor legal liability in class action suits over fraud, which was thought to lead to more "aggressive auditing;" that is, allowing more client accounting manipulation.

Auditing regulations (and accounting oversight in general) have gone through cycles of aggressive and lax enforcement and there is good evidence that the relative oversight influenced corporate and audit behavior. Cassell and Giroux[10] document most of the early postwar period as a high-regulation period and, therefore, associated with less accounting and audit risk. The periods of lax enforcement were 1985–1989 and 1994–2001.

Both were periods of financial and economic euphoria with antiregulatory regimes (under the Reagan and Clinton presidencies). Empirical results support the lower accounting quality (and implied lower audit quality) for these periods[11] Enforcement tightened up somewhat during the H.W. Bush presidency (1989–1993) and, particularly, after the tech crash, major fraud cases including Enron, and the Sarbanes-Oxley Act of 2002. Despite Sarbanes-Oxley much of the 21st century before the subprime meltdown saw continued lax enforcement for the financial sector of the economy.

Lessons to be Learned

After World War II, the level of business corruption gradually increased for a number of mutually reinforcing reasons. Budgets were cut at the SEC and other regulators as business grew and became more complex, but politicians increasingly preferred deregulation—encouraged by an ideological shift and substantial campaign contributions. Business and financial innovations such as derivative pricing, hostile takeovers, structured finance, and junk bonds were introduced and abused. Increased "performance-based" executive compensation drove manipulation incentives. Finally, business culture shifted to increasingly aggressive behavior as more people "got away with it." Particularly important is the significance of continued diligent monitoring and regulatory oversight. Fewer businesspeople get away with it if they are effectively monitored and prosecuted.

CHAPTER 5

Tech Bubble, Bust, and Bankruptcies

Our screens were bathed in red. ... By 11 a.m., the market was dropping faster than Skylab.

—James Cramer

The economy was booming and high-tech companies were changing people's lives. At the start of the 21st century the biggest worry was Y2K, the chance that computers would go bonkers trying to change over to a new millennium, resulting in a crash of all computers and therefore the world economy. This proved a complete dud, either because the techies fixed the problems or no problem really existed. Whatever the answer, the tech bubble continued. The NASDAQ Stock Market (named for the National Association of Securities Dealers Automated Quotations, founded in 1971), where most of the new tech companies traded, rose over 1,000% from 1995 (roughly the start of the tech bubble) to early 2000. That was market euphoria, creating a massive bubble. Greenspan at the Fed was stoking the euphoria with easy money and the Clinton administration was preaching deregulation. Pundits were proclaiming that the economy and markets would continue to rise, while business cycles were a thing of the past. In other words, this was a typical bubble. The market high was reached in early March 2000 with NASDAQ at 5049 on March 10. Then the collapse followed; by late 2002, NASDAQ dropped 80% and the economy was in recession. Recent tech startups were failing in mass, as were many big companies after massive frauds were detected—creating the first financial crisis of the new millennium.

Making the Number

As Mark Twain said, "history doesn't repeat itself, but it rhymes." There were unique features this time. Executive motivations had changed as had finance, a continuing process over several decades. From 1939 to 1951, real executive compensation (adjusted for inflation) fell in part because of high income tax rates.[1] In the early postwar period, tax rates remained high and executives were more interested in perquisites like retirement and health care benefits. Tax reform in the 1980s reduced the top personal income tax rate to 28%, raised in the 1990s to 39.6%, then to 35% in the early 2000s, and back to 39.6% in 2013—this was down from 91% in the 1950s. Capital gains and dividend rates fell to 15%. High-paid executives now had the incentive to increase their compensation—they kept most of the money.

Around 1990, academics were promoting stock options as the best way to motivate chief executive officer (CEO) and other executives—they would now align themselves with stockholders. As an added bonus, the compensation expense associated with stock options did not have to be recorded on the income statement—it seemed to be "free money." Tech company start-ups did not have a lot of extra cash to pay salaries; consequently, they substituted massive amounts of options not just to executives but to almost all employees. The tech companies proved to be either wildly succeeded or crashed and burned. Even low-level workers at an Oracle, Amazon, or eBay could become millionaires—the founders and CEOs, billionaires. Most big and stogy corporations followed suit, giving out piles of options, but miniscule amounts compared to their high-tech counterparts.

Attempting to get tough in the early 1990s, Congress banned corporate tax deductions for executive salary over $1 million. However, compensation based on performance remained unlimited. Compensation includes base salary, cash bonuses, stock options, and other equity-related compensation, plus other benefits such as special pensions. Chief executive officers could now spend considerable time contemplating their own pay—and how it compared to competitors. A well-constructed pay package (that it, as benefiting the executives, not necessarily the corporation) could now bring in tens of millions of dollars to the CEO and under exceptional circumstances hundreds of millions.

The key point became performance, which focused both directly and indirectly on earnings. Cash bonuses typically were (and still are) tied directly to net income, earnings per share (EPS), or other measures of performance. Indirectly, stock options relate to earnings. Options are more likely issued to executives based on past stock price performance, but stock price is expected to follow earnings.

Financial analysts focus on specific companies and industries and make earnings forecasts for the upcoming quarter (and beyond). Institutional Brokers Estimates System and Zacks started compiling analysts' forecasts in the 1970s, followed by First Call. Analyst forecasts became readily available on the Internet by the 1990s. The consensus EPS forecast for each quarter became the number to "meet or beat." Stock prices should continue up as long as earnings are both rising and meeting analyst forecasts. Microsoft, for example, met or beat every quarterly earnings forecast but one for over a decade ending in 1996 and became the most valuable company based on market capitalization—and founder Bill Gates the richest man in the world. Similar results came from General Electric (GE) and other companies about the same time. Failing to meet the analyst forecasts can be a stock price disaster. Both Microsoft and GE fell back to the pack after disappointing earnings during the 21st century.

A high-tech darling with a huge stock price to EPS ratio (PE ratio) can see the stock price plummet on an earnings disappointment, even if the EPS missed by only a penny a share—not good for the company's stock price, particularly not good for CEO compensation. This changed corporate incentives from a long-term focus on success to an immediate focus on this quarter's earnings. It also meant doing just about anything legal to meet forecasts. Because accounting earnings are subject to judgment and estimates, a one cent shortage should be no problem for the enterprising chief financial officer (CFO). Consider Enron as the classic case of incentives gone wrong.

Enron and Special Purpose Entities (SPE)

Enron is the premier scandal of the tech bubble and likely the major fraud case in corporate American history. Two key points in its claim to infamy are that (1) it was big; at its peak the seventh largest American company by market value, $70 billion after huge stock gains, and (2) the fraud and manipulative culture centered at the top—this was not petty crime by mid-level employees. It took over a decade to develop the sophisticated techniques of corruption needed to create a massive culture of deception parading as a high-tech blue chip company.

Enron merits considerable attention because of its sophisticated maneuvering and its use of techniques that have proven to be prominent ever since—including derivatives, market manipulations, SPE, and fair value maneuvering. In addition, there have been a large number of books written by insiders and journalists.[2] Consequently, considerable information is known about the perpetrators, motivations, and specific behavior over the entire history of the company. It took a culture of corruption, an accommodating board of directors, auditor, law firms, banks, the SEC, and other regulators, not to mention political clout maintained by campaign contributions and lobbying. Critics sprung up and were slapped down repeatedly. Basically, Enron embraced all the major components of massive business corruption.

Enron was created as a merger of two gas transmission companies in 1985 and Kenneth Lay soon emerged as CEO and Chairman of the Board, remaining the corporate head throughout. His initial actions suggested executive talent, but ethical lapses and seemingly poor judgment soon emerged. His overall plan was to remake the stogy transmission company into a high-tech conglomerate. This seemed a reasonable plan, except for inept judgment on many issues, misguided incentives of key players, and mass corruption and fraud. The views are still somewhat mixed on whether he tolerated an "overly aggressive behavior" corporate culture versus being fraudster in chief. There is no doubt that his actions were unethical and his conviction for securities fraud and other illegal acts demonstrates criminality. As with many if not most CEOs, his short-term economic incentives encouraged cheating—his cumulative compensation would total hundreds of millions, mainly thanks to massive stock options.

Enron's first fraud happened in 1987, not in Houston, but in a small trading subsidiary in New York City—sham transactions, kickbacks, phony companies, offshore accounts, and the manager skimming millions of dollars. Lay and other executives were not involved in the manipulation, but covered it up rather than face market and regulatory sanctions. Auditor Arthur Andersen investigated the fraud and reported it to the audit committee. Enron, with Andersen's blessing, declared the fraud immaterial, did not report it, and Lay claimed no responsibility. The manager went to jail because of a Justice Department investigation, not thanks to Enron. Lay got away with it, apparently the lesson he learned for future decisions.

Gas Trading and Derivatives

Natural gas pipelines, a highly regulated industry until the late 1980s, were on the list of extraordinarily stodgy low-risk businesses. The strategy was based on long-term contracts, with prices, quantities, and destinations established far into the future. Enron had massive debt, but this was not considered a major problem in a low-risk industry. The ratings agencies were not particularly keen on Enron debt and the company struggled to get and maintain a low investment grade bond rating. That environment changed for the industry and particularly Enron. Gas was on the deregulation to-do list of the Reagan administration. Spot market sales (usually 30-day supply contracts) replaced long-term deals and price volatility spiked. Ken Lay's business strategy changed, shifting focus to a gas trading business. As a market maker, Lay soon looked like a genius. Buyers (mainly utilities) and sellers (mainly drillers) feared this unstable market; they were price takers interested in other aspects of the business. Enron traders became expert middlemen, moving to longer-term contracts as their expertise increased where they could charge a premium over anticipated spot prices. Enron became the major gas trader in North America, the acknowledged expert in the field.

Jeffrey Skilling, a McKinsey consultant, moved to Enron in 1989 to run Enron's Gas Bank, a technique to improve gas market stability by funding drillers in exchange for future gas deliveries—somewhat similar to banks loans, which many drillers were unable to get. Enron could then write long-term contracts with utilities and other users. Skilling's next idea was gas trading based on these long-term contracts—what he called an "asset-light" strategy. This, of course, was in addition to Enron's big pipeline business.

Enron provided derivatives to drillers (suppliers), pipelines, and other users to hedge volatile gas prices, in this case forwards and futures (forwards are buying and selling assets, usually commodities, at a specific price and time in the future, while futures are standardized forwards trading on a formal market). Enron was in the middle, and these lucrative contracts allowed all players (including Enron) to control market risks by hedging. Standardized futures contracts were soon traded on the New York Mercantile Exchange (NYMEX). As the standardized contracts became less lucrative, Enron moved into more complex over-the-counter (OTC) options (the option to buy or sell rather than the commitment) and swaps (such as swapping natural gas for oil).

The easy ability to manipulate derivatives for personal gain (also meaning a higher price or a loss to the counterparty—these are zero-sum-game products) became a predatory strategy and part of the Enron culture. As Enron's trading expanded, so did the use of options, swaps, and various exotic versions often designed to be complex, opaque, possibly deceptive, and profitable. These characteristic made them additional arrows in the quiver of manipulation. Enron traders increasingly speculated in gas and other markets (becoming something of an internal hedge fund), usually quite profitably. When losses struck, they were camouflaged, often using fair value (mark-to-market) to misstate the asset values. It proved to be easy to mislead auditors and regulators about the true value of complex products.

Skilling and Mark-to-Market

Skilling pushed the use of mark-to-market (fair value) accounting for gas trading and received permission from the board and approval from the SEC. The SEC and the Financial Accounting Standards Board (FASB) had been moving toward fair value accounting for financial assets and liabilities, but this was before fair value became generally accepted accounting principles (GAAP) for most financial items. The logic of fair value makes sense for securities that are widely traded and market value easily determined. As part of the fair value process, gains and losses are recognized. Fair value typically "front-loads" income, the rationale being that the actual trade determines profit rather than at the time of delivery and cash collection.[3]

There are downsides to mark-to-market accounting, especially when public market values do not exist. The most critical is the potential for manipulation, particularly in the hands of a deceptive culture like Enron. Many of the long-term gas and other contracts did not have a ready market, especially the various OTC contracts that were inherently more lucrative than trading on NYMEX. Value depended on "mark-to-model," with Enron quantitative experts ("quants") developing the models and determining values to plug into those models. Skilling and other higher-ups could (and did) demand specific gain or loss results for a particular quarter. An increase of two cents in net income to meet analysts' consensus forecasts might require an additional gain of, say, $100,000. The revaluation for each accounting period to the new market value increased earnings volatility (and likely increased the need for further manipulation). Again, income statement numbers were not well connected to cash flows when using fair value.

The SEC approval was mark-to-market for gas contracts. Skilling and Lay expanded fair value across the Enron balance sheet, more or less any asset could be changed to market if needed for earnings manipulation purposes. This did require audit approval and Andersen generally remained accommodating. The SEC also did not review Enron's financial statements vigorously, although the company had a growing record of financial aggressiveness.

Skilling became Enron's Chief Operating Officer in 1996, after Richard Kinder resigned. Kinder believed in earnings management, meeting earnings targets (generally quarterly for meeting EPS forecasts) usually though operating changes to achieve cost savings or any number of accounting gimmicks. The incentives were obvious: executive compensation (especially Lay, Kinder, and Skilling) depended on meeting earnings targets. These executives received piles of options that took years to vest and, as part of the compensation terms, required the executive to continue meeting earnings targets—15% annual earnings growth in addition to meeting or beating earnings forecasts. After Kinder left, Skilling did not hesitate to use increasingly aggressive manipulation tactics.[4]

Fastow's Arrival and SPE

A SPE is a financial arrangement where a separate legal entity (corporation, trust, or partnership) is created for some specific purpose. Various legal details are required including an independent equity investor. First

Boston repackaged General Motors Acceptance Corporation (GMAC) automobile loans in 1985 and used an SPE to hold the securities until they were resold as asset-backed securities—similar to long-term bonds. The repackaging of various standardized consumer bank loans (such as autos, mortgages, or credit card debt) became a common banking practice called "structured finance." The use of SPEs expanded beyond structured finance to serve virtually any specific function that required a separate legal entity. The major advantage was to eliminate assets—and especially liabilities—from the books of the originating company. Of course, from an external analyst's perspective, "off-balance-sheet" accounting screams manipulation.

Given Enron's big debt load, poor bond rating, desire to enter various trading markets and other businesses, plus a penchant for manipulation, SPEs were an obvious choice as a new potential financial weapon. McLean and Elkind[5] summarized Enron's motives as: "keep fresh debt off the books, camouflage existing debt, book earnings, or create operating cash flow." Skilling hired Andrew Fastow, who was working at Continental Illinois Bank as a SPE specialist. Fastow would add his own fraud strategy, well beyond what was asked for or known by the Enron brass.

SPE number one at Enron was a structured finance arrangement called Cactus, created in 1991 to fund the financing of gas and oil drillers using the Gas Bank. Long-term contracts with drillers of $900 million were packaged and sold to GE and others. The purpose was to generate cash and unload the debt to the SPE. Enron formed a partnership with the California Public Employees' Retirement System (CalPERS) in 1993 called JEDI (Joint Energy Development Investments) to acquire drilling and other companies—as a joint venture, this provided the accounting advantages of equity method reporting.[6] When Enron bought out CalPERS interest in 1997, a separate SPE called Chewco was created—keeping the debt off-balance-sheet. However, Fastow could find no one to take the required equity interest (3% of fair value at the time). After being rejected as the "independent investor" by the board, the equity investor became Fastow employee Michael Kopper—an obvious independence violation but accepted by the accommodating auditor and board of directors (the rationale: Kopper was not an officer of Enron). The Chewco deal may have been the start of Fastow's self-serving (and illegal) side deals.

Fastow created LJM (named for Fastow family members Lea, Jeffrey and Michael) in 1999 as a partnership using the SPE structure (LJM2 was created later). The point of LJM was to provide whatever accounting manipulation Enron needed quickly—especially to meet those quarterly earnings targets. Fastow and friends became the independent investors and proceeded to skim off millions in side deals.

Enron bought into several international projects, some energy related and, as Enron had no expertise in such enterprises as water projects, many of these proved idiotic. One strange deal in 1999 was power plants actually floating on barges Enron acquired that ended up on the Nigerian coast. Finding no buyers, Fastow created a sham sale through LJM with Merrill Lynch—it was really a loan. Enron booked a $12 million gain to meet the $1.17 quarterly earnings target. The barges were "bought" back by LJM2 the next year, with the Merrill profit built in.

Enron made a small investment in Rhythms NetConnections, a small Internet company, which went public in 1999 during the bubble period, generating a substantial gain for Enron. To lock in the gain, ill-conceived derivative instruments were used and offset by Enron stock. The complex transactions were fraudulent and bankers from Greenwich NatWest were later indicted for wire fraud—the first of many people caught up by Enron deceptions. Multiple SPEs were created under LJM2, called Raptor I-IV, used to provide various deceptive practices. Fastow added over $200 million to Enron earnings and skimmed millions for himself and co-conspirators. The specifics of Fastow's LJM manipulations apparently were not made clear to executives, the board, or the auditor, especially the nearly $60 million he paid himself from LJM and LJM2.

The Tech Bubble Crashes, So Does Enron

Tech stocks crashed in spring 2000, creating market havoc and a recession. The Raptors were mainly funded by Enron stock (an illicit practice because Enron, in fact, had "no skin in the game," that is, real assets serving as "collateral"), whose price also fell. No further manipulation options were possible. The SPEs were terminated and losses of about $700 million taken. Between this write-down and a multitude of disintegrating businesses, Enron reported a big loss for the third quarter of 2001. Andersen discovered new errors and demanded an addition $1.2 billion write-off of equity and a restatement of earnings from 1997 to 2000. Enron's bond rating was downgraded to junk, which meant no counterparties would trade with Enron except for cash. Rescue attempts were tried; they failed and Enron filed for bankruptcy December 2, 2001. This was the biggest bankruptcy in U.S. history up to that time and unexpected by the investment and Wall Street community. Enron had repeatedly lied about its financial position.

In the aftermath, Congress held hearings, journalists wrote articles and books attempting to explain how this big Wall Street darling could fail so spectacularly, Enron executives paid themselves additional million and fired most of the staff, and criminal investigations and civil lawsuits followed. Fastow was one of the first to be indicted—in addition to his illicit activities for Enron, he also defrauded the company out of millions. He was charged with almost 80 criminal counts, pled guilty, and agreed to a 10-year prison term. Both Skilling and Lay were convicted of multiple felony counts; Lay died before sentencing, while Skilling was sentenced to almost 25 years in jail. In total, over 30 Enron executives and employees were indicted and many jailed.

Giant Frauds: WorldCom, Tyco, Adelphia, and More

Enron was not alone in bad behavior. Bubbles and booms bring out euphoria, increased speculation, and, in an era of huge compensation and profits, greater incentives for manipulation. The 1990s was a decade of continuing emphasis on deregulation. The seemingly perpetually underfunded SEC did a less than adequate job of policing financial reporting of public firms—including Enron. As with the Great Depression, big manipulators crashed in the aftermath of the bursting bubble.

WorldCom

WorldCom has a similar story to Enron, in this case a small, stogy telecommunications company becoming a giant success as a result of government deregulation, and then crashing spectacularly as massive fraud could no longer hide corporate failure; corrupt executives also would be sentenced to long jail sentences. Bernard Ebbers was a founder of Long Distance Discount Services in 1983, after the federal government broke up American Telephone and Telegraph (AT&T) and effectively deregulated long distance phone service. Ebbers became CEO and gobbled up dozens of competitors—working the usual merger manipulation tricks to show spectacular profits. This dinky telco became WorldCom in 1995. The big event was the acquisition of the much larger MCI (for Microwave Communications, Inc.) Communications in 1998.

By the end of 2001, WorldCom had over a hundred billion dollars in assets; however, 2001 net income was $1.5 billion, down from $4.1 billion in 2000. That was not the really bad news. Even the $1.5 billion was fraudulent, discovered by internal audit. It turned out that over $11 billion of operating expenses were capitalized, a simple fraud to book nonexistent earnings (unlike the complex fraud at Enron), originated at the highest levels of the company. These were mainly "line costs," fees to other telecom companies to pay for network access rights—obvious operating expenses. Other fraudulent acts included double counting revenues and unrecorded debt.

Arthur Andersen was WorldCom's auditor; internal auditor Cynthia Cooper, not Andersen, discovered the fraud. Financial statements were restated and Andersen withdrew its 2001 audit opinion. CFO Scott Sullivan was fired and Ebbers resigned. The SEC investigated and WorldCom filed for bankruptcy in mid-2002. WorldCom replaced Enron as the largest bankruptcy in U.S. history. Ebbers was convicted of conspiracy and securities fraud and sentenced to 25 years in prison. Other WorldCom executives also were convicted of various crimes. WorldCom emerged from bankruptcy in 2004 as MCI. The Sarbanes-Oxley Act (SOA) would be passed within a few days of the WorldCom bankruptcy.

Tyco

Tyco Laboratories started as a science research company in 1960 and, after going public, turned itself into a conglomerate. Dennis Kozlowski joined Tyco, rising to CEO in 1992. Mergers became more rapid under Kowlowski, eventually acquiring over 1,000 companies, earnings him the title "Deal-a-Day Dennis." The company became Tyco International in 1993, since Kozlowski viewed the company as a global leader. Tyco excelled in aggressive merger manipulation, the tradition that made conglomerates stock market powerhouses in much of the post–World War II period. The tactics were aggressive enough to cause a SEC investigation in the late 1990s, although Tyco was not charged with fraud.

Tyco's acquisition of CIT Group (a giant commercial finance firm, originally Commercial Investment Trust) became a public road map for merger manipulation when CIT maintained separate financial statements because it had a relatively high credit rating. Tyco made CIT charge off various assets and other adjustments before the acquisition date to give the perception of better performance just after the acquisition (a form of "spring loading" accounting numbers)—CIT reported a loss before the acquisition date and substantial profit and higher revenues just after. Despite the shenanigans, CIT was a bad acquisition when the tech stocks crashed. The subsidiary was sold, netting a $6 billion after-tax loss. Both Kowlowski and CFO Mark Swartz were charged with various fraud-related crimes and other felonies. They were convicted and sentenced to 8–25 years. Tyco settled fraud charges with the SEC and paid $3 billion in class action suits. PricewaterhouseCoopers, Tyco's auditor, paid $225 million in fines. Despite the fraud and lawsuits, Tyco avoided bankruptcy and continues to be listed on the New York Stock Exchange (NYSE). It later split into three companies.

Adelphia

Adelphia was a relatively small company, but deserves special attention for its utter disregard for corporate governance requirements in addition to accounting fraud. John Regas started a local Pennsylvania cable franchise in 1952 and turned it into a communications conglomerate of cable, long-distance phone, and Internet, relying on acquisitions and accumulating massive leverage in the process. Despite massive merger manipulation and various frauds, the company was in trouble by the late 1990s, posting substantial net losses in 1998–2000. The last 10-K was filed for 2000; the company was delisted by NASDAQ. The company restated earnings for 2000 and 2001, in part related to "co-borrowing agreements" with Regas family members using off-balance-sheet affiliates and falsifying statistics. After an SEC investigation of Adelphia and various executives for fraud, the company filed for bankruptcy in June 2002 (about the same time as WorldCom).

The SEC charged Adelphia with hiding billions of dollars of liabilities, falsified earnings, and camouflaging Regas family self-dealings—including some $2.3 billion in loans to various family members. Fraud was rampant, including sham transactions and fraudulent documents. Five of the nine members of the board of directors were John Regas, three sons, and a son-in-law. These family members used Adelphia cash to buy stock, purchase houses, build a golf course, and so on. John was convicted of securities fraud, bank fraud, and conspiracy and sentenced to 15 years in jail. Convictions also came down for other Regas family members and Adelphia executives.

Arthur Andersen

Andersen was the auditor of many ill-fated corporations, not a fraud-committing corporate giant. The federal government considered their actions so heinous that they merited an indictment—a death sentence for an auditor of public clients. After shredding massive amounts of Enron documents (well documented by Houston news as truck load after truck load of shredded documents were hauled off). Forced to surrender its CPA license, the company was soon out of business; the Big Five were down to the Big Four.

Arthur Andersen cofounded his Chicago firm in 1913, built on audit consistency and integrity. It became one of the "Big Eight" audit firms—a term that became popular by the early 1960s for the accounting firms that audited most of the public corporations in America (and increasingly around the world). Audit firms also specialized in tax work and, in the post–World War II period, consulting activities. The auditors became computer experts and developed lucrative computing services. As consulting became the major profit center of the firm, Andersen Consulting split from the rest of the firm in 1989. (Andersen Consulting became the largest consulting firm in the world and changed its name to Accenture.)

With Andersen Consulting gone, revenues were reduced and hard to maintain; the company found it difficult to compete in an increasingly competitive market. Audits became more "aggressive," meaning the company was increasingly willing to audit difficult and manipulative clients and more accommodating to their needs. Barbara Toffler, a former Andersen partner in charge of ethics, summed it up: "in the new world, clients had become too valuable to defy. The distortion of the 'Tradition' now meant you could best serve the client—and therefore, keep the client—by keeping it happy. ... The worst possible sin you could commit at Arthur Andersen, I learned the hard way, was to upset the client—even if they desperately needed to hear the bad news."[7] The result was Andersen became the auditor giving clean opinions to one audit-scandal-corporation after another. Sunbeam and Waste Management were major late-1990s frauds and Andersen paid millions to settle stockholder lawsuits. The really big ones were Enron and WorldCom—both considered by Andersen as among the "most important clients" according to Toffler.

It is little wonder that the Justice Department had little patience with Andersen and saw the document-destroying episode as an outrage. Andersen was convicted of obstruction of justice. Lawsuits followed. Although the conviction was reversed by the Supreme Court in 2005, it was too late to save Andersen. Several pundits predicted that other firms deserved to be indicted, but none were—possibly because they were now "too big to fail."

And More

The early 21st century, like the 1930s, uncovered widespread manipulation, corruption, and fraud. Accounting write-offs and earnings restatements became commonplace, often in the billions of dollars. SEC investigations and class action lawsuits often followed. Cisco Systems wrote down $2.8 billion in inventory in 2001 on take-or-pay supply contracts. JDSU (originally JDS Uniphase, the merger of JDS Fitel and Uniphase) wrote off $40 billion in goodwill and long-term assets in 2001. Xerox restated $6 billion in earnings in 2002 after inflating revenues over the previous five years. Bristol-Myers-Squibb also overstated earnings (by $2 billion). Quest Communications overstated revenues in 2002 and was subject to SEC and Justice Department investigations associated with "hollow swaps." AOL-Time Warner (after the merger of America Online and Time-Warner) wrote off $54 billion in goodwill from the disastrous merger (the total loss for the year, 2002, was almost $100 billion). Various banks and other financial institutions had multiple legal problems with predatory practices, securities analysts' deceptive stock analysis, and assorted misdemeanors. Imclone Systems CEO Samuel Waksal was jailed for insider trading; the case made national headlines when Martha Stewart was investigated for insider trading when informed by Waksal to sell and convicted of lying.

Even this expanded list represents only the tip of the corruption iceberg flow, but represents the bigger icebergs. In a 2002 study the General Accounting Office(GAO) (GAO, later called the Government Accountability Office) analyzed 919 earnings restatements from 845 public companies from 1997 to 2002. Restatements were almost unheard of through the 1980s and suggest the substantial drop in earnings quality and growing use of manipulation during the booming 1990s. The biggest category was revenue recognition problems, almost 40% of the total. Included in the GAO's list were 80 Standard & Poor's (S&P) 500 companies, about 16% of the total. Tice and Tse (2013) identified 8,859 restatements over the 10-year period 2000 and 2009.

The Sarbanes-Oxley Act

Congress held hearing after many of the accounting scandals in the 1970s and 1980s, issuing reports and calls for reform. Such was also the case after Enron's bankruptcy in December of 2002. Perhaps a dozen special committees in both the House and Senate pontificated mightily as Enron executives and other bit players stonewalled as the news cameras rolled. The Senate Banking Committee under Senator Paul Sarbanes (Democrat from Maryland) proved to be the most important, laying out a foundation for legislation based on specific problems, including audit problems, weak corporate governance, and a poorly funded SEC.

Legislation more or less died in committee, in part because Congressman Michael Oxley (Republican from Ohio), Chairman of the House Committee on Financial Services, was less interested in massive reform. (After he retired from Congress in 2007, Oxley became a lobbyist for the Financial Industry Regulatory Authority, affiliated with the securities industry.) Then WorldCom went bankrupt (and several other scandals and bankruptcies occurred around the same time, such as Adelphia) in mid-2002. Legislation quickly followed this renewed outrage and the SOX of 2002 passed and was signed into law by the end of July. Thanks to WorldCom, SOX included a fairly stringent reform package.

SOX is by far the biggest regulatory reform in financial markets, financial disclosure, and auditing since the original 1930s securities acts. Particularly important are major changes to corporate governance requirements, the creation of the Public Company Accounting Oversight Board (PCAOB) and other audit-related rules, and new responsibilities of CEOs and CFOs. SOX also affected SEC requirements, FASB funding, and stock exchange rules. Various parts of the bill came under attack, mainly by corporations and their various supporters, in large part because of perceived huge additional compliance costs. The standard argument was used: the expected benefits did not justify the costs.

Corporate Governance

Corporate governance became a major area for reform. The potential for corruptions expands exponentially when governance is weak, accommodating, or part of the manipulation. Such was the case at Adelphia, when Regas family board members used their fiefdom as a convenient automatic teller machine. Virtually all of the scandal-plagued companies suffered from weak governance or worse. After the debacles at Enron, Adelphia, and all the rest, governance became a substantial concern of Congress.

The objectives of the board of directors are long-term strategic planning and oversight of the company's business strategy and operations. Corporate governance is the overall structure in place to promote these objectives. The majority of big corporations are run by a dominant leader who is both chairman of the board and CEO. Consequently, the CEO typically was in position to control the board and ensure that board members were allies. Researchers in economics and business have analyzed governance for decades, providing evidence of preferred practices. Findings suggest a well-functioning board should be made up primarily of diligent outsiders preferably not buddies of the CEO, the audit committee of the board should have substantial power in picking and reviewing the results of the audits, and substantial disclosure should be made related to board and executive compensation, information on the board members to be elected (preferably all should be elected annually), board committee results (audit, compensation, executive, and so on), and thorough information on amendments up for stockholder votes.

New corporate governance rules were part of SOX, which included some guidance but also shifted responsibility to the stock exchanges and SEC oversight. The NYSE and NASDAQ rewrote governance guidelines including the need for the majority of the board members to be independent, and various rules on the major committees—compensation, audit, etc.—which would be composed exclusively of independent directors.

Particularly important to investors and analysts are the expanded SEC disclosure requirements in the proxy statement. The members of the board up for election are listed with a short biography. Most companies require annual election for all members; however, because they generally run unopposed, the important point is to determine the relative competence of the members. The members of board committees and board member compensation also are disclosed, along with committee responsibilities. Reasonable details of the audit committee are described, including fees paid to the external auditor, the auditor selection process, and information on auditor/audit committee meetings and interactions.

An analysis of compensation paid to the major executives is detailed, listing base pay, bonuses, stock-based compensation, retirement funding, and various perquisites and other benefits. Some discussion is usually presented on the relationship of compensation and corporate performance. SOX does not limit executive compensation, but current SEC rules do provide considerable information. Because the executive incentives remain basically the same as before SOX, the potential to manipulate accounting numbers remains virtually unchanged. The concept of "performance-based compensation" does not seem to eliminate big pay packages for mediocre or worse performance. Each company's compensation committee determines how performance is to be measured. Additional rules were added by the Dodd-Frank Act, described in the next chapter.

Audit Requirements and Additional Reports

The audit committee is responsible for both external and internal audits. Auditors are hired and paid by the corporations (now through the audit committee). Therefore, the auditor incentives remain to be as accommodating as possible. The audit committee must be made up exclusively of independent board members and the committee chair must be a "financial expert," with expertise on GAAP, audit preparation, and internal controls. That may provide some assurance; however, the various financial and accounting scandals both before and after SOX suggest continued concern.

The auditor's report (also called the audit opinion) is included in the 10-K, usually at the start of the financial statement section. Almost all opinions are clean (which are called "unqualified opinions" and include: "the statements present fairly the financial position and results of operations … in accordance with GAAP"). The date of the opinion indicates when the audit was completed and is listed on the audit report. Presumably, an early date suggests a problem-free audit. The SEC requires the 10-K to be issued to the SEC within 60 days of the end of the fiscal year, which means the audit must be completed quickly. Any 10-Ks submitted after this 60-day limit suggests severe accounting/auditing problems.[8]

SOX requires addition reports from executives and the auditor. Both the CEO and CFO of corporations must certify that each 10-K and 10-Q under Section 302: "fairly presents, in all material respects, the financial condition and results of operations of the issuer." A later section of SOX describes severe penalties for failure to comply ("willfully providing false information" or "providing false information" could results in jail time up to 20 years and million dollar fines). Consequently, increased executive incentives exist not to commit fraud. In theory at least, chief executives at companies like Enron could not claim ignorance. It turned out that conviction proved to be difficult. Soon after SOX the CEO of HealthSouth was indicted but not convicted in what seemed to be a clear cut violation of Section 302.

Internal controls represent the procedures to direct corporate resources, including measurement and monitoring. Internal control has been an integral part of auditing for decades and a federal requirement since the foreign Corrupt Practices Act of 1977. The Treadway Commission (National Commission on Fraudulent Financial Reporting) began in 1985 to study fraud and their findings included an internal control framework.

Section 401 of SOX proved to be the biggest problem in regulatory enforcement shortly after SOX (regulatory overreach and onerous audit costs to comply according to the critics, who included most public corporations and the Chamber of Commerce). Section 401 requires that both the auditor and company must submit reports on internal control as part of the 10-K, particularly pointing out any "material weaknesses" discovered. Media coverage on post-SOX audits was intense, which encouraged companies to submit to greater audit scrutiny (and considerably higher costs). The greater audit time involved in these audits caused the Big Four to drop a number of audit clients (generally smaller public companies and likely those with lower accounting quality), which were picked up by non-Big Four auditors.[9] The high cost of compliance was the early complaint, relative to the perception of few benefits, including "over-auditing" in the field and over-regulation by the SEC. Analysts and other outsiders generally assumed that because internal control requirement had been in place for decades it was unlikely that major corporations could be substandard or need much additional audit time.

In *Earnings Magic and the Unbalance Sheet,*[10] I evaluated the auditors' internal control reports for the 30 companies in the Dow Jones Industrial Average shortly after SOX. These are the bluest of the blue chip corporations of America. Even in this group, material weaknesses were found for two companies, American Insurance Group (AIG) and GE, both firms that had AAA bonds ratings and later fell from grace during the 2008 mortgage debacle. Both were required to restate earnings. Derivative accounting was the problem at GE—this conglomerate has a major finance subsidiary, GE Credit, with a large derivative operation. AIG had multiple problems, including "control environment, controls over evaluation of risk transfer, controls over balance sheet reconciliation, controls over accounting for certain derivative transactions, and controls over income tax accounting." AIG, of course, became one of the big losers in 2008 (as were the taxpayers forced to bail out the company).

Regulatory Funding

A great way to make regulation effectiveness go away is to eliminate, or at least substantially reduce, funding. Without much of a budget, it is difficult to do a competent job. That had sometimes been the fate of the SEC as funding has gone up and down as presidential administrations changed. Those favoring deregulation (common since the Reagan revolution of the 1980s) have seen falling budgets. The SEC's roles were expanded without expanded budgets. The 1990s saw tremendous economic and corporate growth, especially the new high-tech companies that went public well before profits emerged. The SEC focused on these problematic companies, to the detriment of persistent reviews of 10-Ks and other financial reports. Enron was the most prominent neglected example.

One of the regulatory fixes of SOX was better funding for the SEC, FASB, and brand new PCAOB. SEC funding, a federal appropriation, increased substantially—at least in the short run. Prior to SOX, the FASB was on its own, raising money from contributions (much of it from corporations and corporate-sponsored organizations—leading to conflicts of interest) and selling copies of pronouncements and other stuff. SOX allows the FASB to receive "support fees" from public companies based on corporate market value. Basically, the FASB draws up a budget (with SEC approval) and bills the corporations for their share. PCAOB funding works the same way. The concept is that adequate funding will be maintained and both organizations will remain independent and free of corporate conflicts.

PCAOB

Historically, auditing standards (GAAS) were created by committees of the American Institute of Certified Public Accounting (AICPA), essentially the trade association for CPAs. This was the group that had the expertise, but also self-interest in promoting themselves. SOX replaced this with the PCAOB as a semi-public nonprofit organization. Both public companies and the auditors must register with the PCAOB. The five-member board is chosen by the SEC to serve five-year terms (and can be appointed for a second term, but no more).

The PCAOB issues auditing standards; in addition to that, auditors are inspected for audit quality, with the power to institute disciplinary actions after appropriate investigations for violating the law and professional standards. In 2003 the PCAOB adopted various existing standards as "interim." As of 2013 the regulator issued a total of 16 auditing standards, all approved by the SEC. In addition the PCAOB issued ethics and independence rules, quality control standards, attestation standards, plus "audit practice alerts and other guidance." The organization's website (pcaobus. org) also lists "current standard-setting and related rulemaking activities."

The PCAOB inspects the audit firms to "assess compliance with the Sarbanes-Oxley Act, the rules of the Board, the rules of the SEC, and professional standards in connection with the firm's performance of audits, issuance of audit reports, and related matters involving U.S. companies, other issues, brokers, and dealers" (pcaobus.org.inspections/pages/default. aspx). The initial inspections were made on the Big 4 by 2004. The auditors that issue reports on at least 100 firms must be inspected annually; all others, within three years. There were nine auditors inspected annually in 2012, including Big 4 Deloitte & Touche, Ernst & Young, KPMG, and PricewaterhouseCoopers, plus BDO Seidman, Crowe Horwath, Grant Thornton, MaloneBailey, and McGladrey & Pullen. The inspection reports are listed on the Board's website.

The Board has the authority to: "investigate and discipline registered public accounting firms and person associated with those firms for non-compliance." The process includes investigations, hearings, sanctions, and disciplinary orders. Settled disciplinary orders by auditor are listed, a total of 50 in 2013, including Deloitte & Touche in 2007, Pricewaterhouse-Coopers in 2011, and Ernst & Young in 2012.

The Board is funded by the audited public corporations. The PCAOB prepares a budget, which must be approved by the SEC and the total cost is charged to the public companies as "accounting support fees" based on the total market capitalization of those over $25 million. The 2013 budget was set at $245.6 million, an 8% increase over the 2012 budget, with an increasing number of international inspections and implementing a new broker-dealer inspection program given as the primary reasons for the increase.

Manipulation Continues

With a better funded SEC after SOX, a chastened audit industry subject to a new regulator, bankrupt companies with leaders facing severe prison time, and companies with considerably more governance, audit and disclosure requirements, scandals should have dropped close to zero. But no. Scandals continued until (and beyond) the big one—subprime loan in 2008. HealthSouth was a major fraud uncovered in 2003. Dozens of stock options scandals were uncovered mid-decade. Several frauds were discovered, including various financial firms well before the subprime meltdown. The biggest one was Bernard Madoff's Ponzi scheme, uncovered about the time that the world economy was in crisis in late 2008.

HealthSouth

HealthSouth was the country's largest inpatient rehabilitation health facility at the start of the new millennium, founded by Richard Scrushy in the 1980s. Once again, mergers provided both massive growth and merger manipulation magic. Healthcare, especially Medicare and other government programs, allowed inpatient care providers substantial opportunities to cheat and Scrushy and Co. became manipulation specialists. HealthSouth was eventually charged by Medicate with illegally inflating billings, after which profits dropped and other providers piled on with lawsuits and charges of fraud. The company was forced to restate $2.5 billion in earnings and the SEC charged the company and executives with accounting fraud. Stock trading in the NYSE was suspended and the bond rating down-grading to low junk status. The Justice Department charged securities, wire and mail fraud, as well as money laundering.

Several executive pled guilty and testified against Scrushy, who became the first CEO charged for knowingly filing false reports with the SEC under the SOX Section 302 provisions. Amazingly, he was acquitted. He did have to pay SEC fines and settle stockholder lawsuits. Justice was apparently done when he was later convicted of bribery in a completely different case and sentenced to seven years in prison. HealtchSouth avoided bankruptcy, reorganized, and regained its listing on the NYSE.

Stock Option Maneuvering

Stock options have been a major driver in CEO compensation since the 1990s and probably the prime motivator for corporate manipulation. The amazing gains available proved not enough for many companies, who invented new ways to cheat in the form of "backdating" and "spring loading." After stock options were approved by the board (which legally sets the option-granting date), many companies falsified the grant date to a date earlier than legally granted, usually the lowest stock price of the period when stock prices were lower, which increased to amount of gain to the holder—it also reduced the amount of cash to be paid to the company. The practice violated SEC disclosure requirements, accounting and tax laws. The SEC investigated over 140 companies and filed civil charges against 24; about 150 companies restated earnings based on internal investigations of backdating.[11]

Spring loading happens when options are granted immediately before good news (basically a form of enrichment based on insider information). Another form of this move was issuing options after very bad news and stock drops—186 companies handed out options just after 9/11. Finally was the practice of "exercise backdating," backdating after options have been exercised to a lower stock price. The SEC investigated over 100 companies related to stock option maneuvering. The usual defense claim was ignorance of the rules.

Another interesting form of manipulation was "speed vesting." Using their new-found independence after SOX provided funding directly from public companies, the FASB required companies to record the value of stock options granted on their income statements as compensation expense beginning in 2006. (Prior to that, the option compensation expense had to be disclosed in a footnote but expensing was not required.) To avoid the added expense in 2006, many companies had them vest in 2005, speed vesting. This was not illegal, but frustrated investors and analysts hoping for greater accounting honesty and fewer greedy executives.

Financial Scandals

Major manipulation at Enron included the abuse of both SPEs and derivatives. Both of these instruments continued to be means of abuse and the financial industry was a master misusing both. Evidence for this showed up well before 2008. Fannie Mae, the quasi-governmental (called a government-sponsored entity or GSE) buyer of mortgages, with a set of special provisions to reduce expenses (including a line of credit from the Treasury Department and special tax breaks), relentlessly used its political clout and weak oversight to enrich the company (e.g., expanding allowable leverage) and especially its senior executives. In 2004 Fannie suffered from weak internal control and was forced to restate earnings by $9 billion because of faulty derivative valuations; excessively compensated CEO Franklin Raines and CFO Timothy Howard were fired. AIG accounted for reinsurance improperly and overstated stockholders' equity $1.7 billion. The company also paid fines to the SEC and Justice Department for incorrectly accounting for insurance deals. Both companies proved to be big-time losers in the 2008 financial crisis.

The mutual fund industry was investigated by then New York Attorney General Eliot Spitzer in 2003, mainly associated with late trading and market timing. Mutual fund prices are set every day after market trading closes. Buy and sell order received after market closing had to wait to the end of the next business day to be executed. Various mutual fund companies were executing late orders after market closing for "select customers." Because only these traders had full information on market prices, this was considered unfair. The mutual funds booked the entries to appear as if the trades had been received before market closing. Following Spitzer, the SEC found additional abuses, including another form of "front-running," in this case by providing select customers and employees insider information about expected price movements based on block trading (buying or selling large blocks of stock) the mutual funds were expected to do. The tipped-off customers would then buy or sell in front of the block trade.[12] The settlement involved large fines rather than jail time for the perpetrators.

Lessons to be Learned

Enron was America's major (and most infamous) business scandal, but with several close competitors in the 21st century. At the time, Enron paid top-dollar for executive talent. Detailed annual financial reports were submitted. Accounting standards were in place, as were many levels of monitoring and oversight. How could an outrageous, complex fraud continue for years with few people even recognizing a possible problem could exist? Apparently, the potential rewards for cheating were too great to resist, while oversight proved ineffective. Enron, of course, was not unique. High-level manipulation at major companies was pervasive. Unfortunately, Enron, WorldCom and most of the rest had to blow themselves up before the frauds were discovered.

The response seemed right on, detailed public hearings and media scrutiny, followed by the major reform bill, Sarbanes-Oxley—the most significant regulatory reform since the 1930s. It was long and complicated and involved major overhauls of auditing, corporate governance, and increasing responsibilities for the SEC (along with substantial budget increases) and the creation of the PCAOB. However, other areas of concern remained uncorrected, the most important being the uncontrolled executive compensation fueling future incentives to cheat. Areas of particular concern to the financial industries (structured finance, SPEs, derivatives, captured financial regulators) also remained and these would explode into a gigantic world-wide crisis in just a few year.

CHAPTER 6

Subprime Meltdown and Beyond

Those who argued for deregulation contend ... that the real cost of regulation is the stifling of innovation. The sad truth is that in America's financial markets, innovations were directed at circumventing regulations, accounting standards, and taxation. They created products that were so complex, they had the effect of both increasing risk and information asymmetries.

When there are important agency problems and externalities, markets typically fail to produce efficient outcomes—contrary to the widespread belief in the efficiency of markets. This is one of the rationales for financial market regulation.

—Joseph Stiglitz

Economic euphoria has been around since Tulip Mania in 17th-century Holland and the South Sea bubble in 18th-century England. Subprime proved to be another classic case of capitalism gone mad. Housing is basically one of the most stable asset classes around, not easily subject to bubbles, at least on a national scale. Prospective homeowners typically put 20% down and are subject to a rigorous credit analysis to determine if they are financially fit. Regulators are seemingly everywhere and Fannie Mae and Freddie Mac (government-sponsored enterprises or GSEs) have been around for decades to ensure a liquid market. This should be a robust model for financial stability.

Despite this description of a stable market, housing and mortgages exploded, mortgage brokers and Wall Street banks turned this market into a predatory casino, and the massive mortgage/structured finance/derivative/overleveraged bubble collapsed in 2008. In addition to the obvious villains making money from this mess, it took the other players—Federal

Reserve and other federal regulators, rating agencies, auditors, attorneys, and investors—to make the bubble inflate. Accountants, auditors, and accounting regulators played supporting roles, but were still participants in the unfolding corruption and manipulation.

Mortgage Abuse and Fraud

The housing market in the post–World War II period was a hodgepodge of government and commercial interests, with conflicting incentives and institutions gaming the system. The depression-era New Deal created new institutions to stabilize housing and mortgage markets after collapsing real estate prices and millions of foreclosures. Legislation created the Federal Home Loan Bank Board (1932) encouraging mortgages issued through federally insured thrifts, the Home Owners' Loan Corporation (1933) established to replace home mortgages in or near default; the National Housing Act set up the Federal Housing Administration (FHA, 1934) to provide an improved real estate financing system, the 1937 U.S. Housing Act created the United States Housing Authority (now Department of Housing and Urban Development, HUD) to clear slums and build low-rent housing, while the Federal National Mortgage Association (Fannie Mae) was created in 1938 to establish a secondary mortgage market. Home ownership and financing has been public policy ever since. These programs provided a reasonably effective but cumbersome system and home ownership rose from about 40% to over 60% by mid-century.

A policy issue was the use of "redlining" as a form of "commercial segregation," with minorities viewed as uncreditworthy and denied mortgages or charged higher ("subprime") rates without much regard for credit history or income. In response to this practice, the Fair Housing Act of 1968 outlawed redlining and the Community Reinvestment Act of 1977 banned certain discriminatory mortgage practices. Programs to expand home ownership (and in the process increase subprime lending) were instituted by both the Clinton and later Bush administrations.

Fannie Mae was "privatized" in 1968 as a public corporation, with special privileges of a GSE. The Government National Mortgage Corporation (Ginnie Mae) and the Federal Home Loan Mortgage Corporation (Freddie Mac) were created as GSEs about the same time. A problem with privatization of Fannie Mae and the others was that they became public corporations subject to the same incentives of maximizing profits (for executives as well as investors) as any other corporation—not conducive to a public function. With their political clout, the GSEs were in position to game the system, which they did masterfully.

The debt securities issued by the GSEs, initially out-of-favor because borrowers could pay back principal any time, became increasingly acceptable as they seemed to be "guaranteed" by the federal government with higher interest rates than Treasury securities. A whole set of factors converged to create a massive mortgage machine. These included the creation of asset-backed securities (ABSs) that included mortgages, auto loans, and credit card balance; investment banks developing new techniques to make the ABSs desirable to investors (and increasingly profitable to the banks), bond-rating agencies with defective credit models and the desire for revenue giving out undeserved investment-grade ratings, cognitively captured federal agencies that apparently considered themselves subsidiaries of the banks and fostered banking interests rather than public interests, politicians promoting home ownership for subprime borrowers and benefits to GSEs and banks, and also the GSEs promoting their own investor interests rather the public benefits, and an increasingly predatory mortgage-finance industry. All these diverse parts had to fit into place and they did.

The Securitization Machine

Structured finance (the process is called securitization) means bundling standard financial assets such as auto loans, mortgages, or credit card balances into pooled assets that are resold as the equivalent of long-term bonds, ABSs. The investors get the cash from interest and principal payments and the underlying financial assets serve as collateral. A bank can originate, say, mortgages and/or buy mortgages from mortgage lenders and pool them into mortgage-backed securities (MBSs). The first MBSs were created by HUD in 1970. The private sector, mainly Wall Street investment banks, began creating ABSs in the 1980s, soon after the savings and loan industry was deregulated and ready to sell mortgages, take in jumbo certificates of deposit and buy high-yielding financial assets.

Conceptually, structured finance promotes liquidity by creating products that can be sold to bond investors globally, diversifies risk with potentially thousands of mortgages or other financial assets, and allows investors to determine the level of risk they are willing to tolerate by selling ABSs in tranches (slices) based on relative risk. Banks discovered that their normally illiquid assets holdings such as mortgages or car loans could be converted to cash at a profit and new investments made. Mortgage companies and other financial firms expanded or found new markets and created a huge mortgage machines to feed the growing demand for mortgage origination.

Salomon Brothers was the mortgage expert in the 1980s and jumped into the private MBS market as the major player. This was the investment bank that really created investor demand to buy MBSs despite their problems (including very long maturities and the ability of mortgagees to liquidate mortgages at any time). The other banks jumped into the market. Bear Stearns created a vertically integrated mortgage operation from mortgage originators (buying Encore Credit and EMC Mortgage) to Bear-sponsored hedge funds focusing on debt instruments. Bear's hedge funds collapsed in 2007 and the company was the first to avoid bankruptcy only with a government bailout.

Moody's, Standard & Poor's, and the other bond rating agencies turned rating ABSs into major profit centers (rising to about 40% of Moody's 2006 profit). Armed with statistical rating models that included only the most recent years and no mechanism in their equations to consider the possibility that real estate prices could go down, they accommodated the banks that issued ABS with investment grade ratings. As stated by McLean and Nocera[1] "Moody's and the other rating agencies turned their backs on their own integrity." The lowest risk tranches of MBSs and other ABSs got AAA ratings (Standard & Poor's highest credit quality rating), considered more or less equivalent to U.S. Treasuries and the handful of corporations also receiving AAA ratings. With higher yields than Treasuries, pension funds, insurance companies, and other investors around the world jumped into this market with enthusiasm and little due diligence.

A major issue was the growing prevalence of predatory mortgage lending. Founded in 1969, Countrywide was initially relatively conservative.

When Angelo Mozilo became chief executive early in the 21st century, he focused on market share and profit. Under Mozilo's aggressive leadership, the company became the biggest mortgage finance company, originating about 20% of America's mortgages by 2006. Subprime loans were very lucrative and predatory practices abundant in this market. With growing demand and lack of federal regulatory oversight (partly based on lobbying and various benefits given to politicians such as low-interest mortgages), less and less attention was paid to proper documentation or any quality control requirements. Countrywide was basically bankrupt by 2007 and acquired by Bank of America. Mozilo was charged by the Securities and Exchange Commission (SEC) with securities fraud and insider trading, paying fines close to $70 million. Bank of America would ultimately pay billions of dollars to settle various lawsuits associated with Countrywide's predatory practices.

Bubble and Collapse

The national housing market had been remarkably stable for decades. Economist Robert Shiller demonstrated that over the last century housing prices roughly kept up with inflation; however, from 1990 housing prices doubled by 2006. When housing prices peaked around 2006 the housing bubble was doomed. As long as prices were rising, buyers not able to make mortgage payments could sell or just borrow more money based on the higher collateral values. After that, only illicit practices could be used to maintain the bubble machine.

The securities machine continued—as paraphrased from Citigroup chief executive officer (CEO) Chuck Prince: "as long as the music's playing, you've got to keep dancing." Lending practices became more predatory, banks repackaged MBSs that did not sell (mainly those with lower bond ratings) into collateralized debt obligations (CDOs) and sold those (after getting the bond-raters seal of approval of investment grade ratings—many tranches still AAA). Mortgage originators started going bankrupt, MBS and CDO investors were harder to find, and bankers started to realize that the bust was on. Some bankers came to the realization in time to attempt to get out of the mortgage market and/or hedge using credit default swaps (CDS) (CDSs, derivatives that paid off if the security defaulted).

Famously, hedge fund manager John Paulson made billions mainly using CDSs to speculate against the CDO bubble and Goldman Sachs also was well hedged to mitigate losses. Other banks (including Lehman Brothers and Citigroup whose CEOs were apparently still dancing) were too late to sell out or hedge—these markets dried up by 2008. The highly leveraged banks had portfolios of what was now realized as junk MBSs and CDOs on their books and recorded substantial losses (the rating agencies were now downgrading these securities), little or no liquidity, and limited ability to borrow in the short-term credit markets—the combination of illiquidity and insolvency. First up was Bear Stearns, the smallest and weakest of the five big investment banks. Bear's collapse was the first major catastrophe in the subprime crisis.

Bear Collapse

In March 2008 the crisis struck; investors would not refinance Bear's short-term loans, mainly repurchase agreements. As the bank most vested in the mortgage machine, Bear was the most vulnerable financially as this market panicked. Bear had only $12 billion in equity to cover $395 billion in assets in 2007 (a leverage ratio over 30 times), meaning a 3% drop in asset value wipes out equity. Later analysis by J.P. Morgan identified billions of dollars of "toxic assets" on Bear's books (meaning massive losses based on fair value). Simultaneously, Bear had over $100 billion in repurchase agreements—short-term liabilities; the strategy was to borrow using cheap short-term debt to invest in longer-term, high return assets. Moody's downgraded much of Bear's debt on March 10, causing Bear's trading partners to stop overnight funding and demand cash for common transactions.

At the last minute, Treasury Secretary Hank Paulson and Federal Reserve chairman Ben Bernanke intervened. Fed cash allowed Bear to survive into the weekend in anticipation of finding a big bank to acquire Bear. J.P. Morgan was an obvious suitor, but Morgan auditors discovered $30 billion in mortgage-backed junk it was not willing to assume. Only when the federal government agreed to assume most of the losses on these toxic assets would Morgan agree to the last-minute deal. Thus, the first bank was saved from bankruptcy, but only after a massive government bailout.

The Bubble Collapses

The subprime meltdown continued as banks and other financials recorded multibillion dollar write-downs in mid-2008. Various financial organizations imploded. The giant GSEs, Fannie Mae and Freddie Mac, held or insured about half the U.S. mortgages in 2008, some $5–6 trillion worth and backed up with very little equity—which was falling as they recorded billion dollar losses. They were not exactly bailed out, but taken over by the federal government in early September—as the Federal Housing Finance Agency (the GSE's new regulatory) put them in conservatorship. The stockholders were basically wiped out and much of senior management terminated. Treasury poured billions of dollars into Fannie and Freddie in exchange for preferred stock (paying a 10% dividend plus warrants to buy 79.9% of their common) to backstop their mortgage holdings with equity and help stabilize the financial markets. The Fed also bought substantial amounts of Fannie and Freddie securities as part of "quantitative easing."[2]

The other major investment banks had similar if less severe problems to Bear with only three obvious solutions: (1) major equity investment or takeover by anyone with big bucks, (2) federal bailouts, or (3) bankruptcy. Because these banks were counterparties on literally millions of contracts, bankruptcy was an option to avoid—a "too big to fail" problem. The two biggest investment banks arranged for capital infusions. Warren Buffet's Berkshire Hathaway acquired $5 billion in Goldman preferred stock, while Mitsubishi invested $9 billion in Morgan Stanley. Both Goldman and Morgan accepted the Fed's offer of becoming bank holding companies and thus subject to Federal Reserve largesse (and regulation). Merrill Lynch was acquired by Bank of America—an acquisition Bank of America would later regret. That left Lehman Brothers as the odd bank out.

Lehman avoided a Bear moment until September, just after the seizure of Fannie and Freddie. Lehman was also highly leveraged (assets to equity of over 26 times in 2006) and relied on short-term borrowing. Like Bear, Lehman was a major MBS player. As MBS and CDO securities got harder to dispose of in 2007–2008, more and more of the remaining MBS/CDO securities were dumped into off-shore Special Purpose

Entities (SPEs) (i.e., off-balance-sheet). Lehman announced a quarterly loss of $3.9 billion on September 10, 2008 (after a $2.8 billion loss the previous quarter). The rest of the financial market refused to deal with Lehman and a run on the bank was on. The team of Paulson, Bernanke, and New York Fed Chairman Tim Geitner were reunited to save Lehman. The options: a buyout of Lehman assets by a "liquidation consortium," an acquisition partner, or bankruptcy.[3] British bank Barclays was a likely candidate, but had no interest without a big federal bailout similar to Bear. Paulson and partners refused and Lehman failed September 15, the largest bankruptcy in American history.

Within days of the Lehman failure, insurance giant American Insurance Group (AIG) was in trouble. AIG's insurance subsidiaries were in decent shape, but the company bet heavily on CDSs, a derivative resembling insurance.[4] AIG apparently viewed CDSs as another category of insurance with little risk and held $560 billion (at face or notional value) in CDSs by the end of 2007. AIG was a major counterparty to Lehman and bond rating agencies almost immediately downgraded the company from AAA to A—a major hit to investors interested in AIG short-term debt or even insurance. Potentially even worse, AIG was a counterparty to most major banks and the largest insurance provider in the country. On September 17, the Fed bailed out AIG with $85 billion in a "secured credit facility" (increased to $180 billion by early 2009). AIG had a net loss approaching $100 billion for 2008 and the stock price crashed to 35¢ early in 2009 (from over $70) a share.

The battle to save the financial world was on. The credit markets basically froze up as all financial players had no idea who was insolvent or what the government would do; after all, bailouts were no longer a near certainty after Lehman. In fact, the Fed, Treasury and other federal agencies would pour in trillions of dollars to make sure no other financial giant failed. Step one was to reintroduce liquidity into the credit markets, beginning with money market funds. A major money market fund, Reserve Primary Fund, "broke the buck" by reducing share value from $1 to 97¢. Investors, no longer believing money market funds completely safe, created a run on Reserve (which liquidated) and moved large sums out of all money market funds.

The Fed established various "funding facilities" to provide massive liquidity into the financial system. First up was the Commercial Paper Funding Facility in October 2008 used to purchase commercial paper to maintain that market and assist money market funds as major buyers. The Term Asset-Backed Securities Loan Facility started in November to loan short-term funds to banks, which were allowed to use ABSs as collateral. Other programs followed in 2009. The fed funds rate was lowered to 1% by the end of October, pumping cash into the banking system. By the end of the year the Fed introduced its zero interest rate policy to drop the fed funds rate to 0–0.25%. Banks could now get cash for essentially nothing, while money market and other short-term investors could expect a near-zero return.

The Fed suffered considerable criticism from politicians, pundits, and economists. Former Fed Chair Paul Volcker pointed out the Fed went to "the very edge of its lawful and implied powers, transcending certain long embedded central banking principles and practices." Economist Anna Schwartz was even more critical, calling the action "a rogue operation … The Fed had no business intervening here."[5] The total cost to the federal government for the multiple bailout programs was in the trillions of dollars. Neil Barofsky, the former Special Inspector General in Charge of Oversight of Troubled Asset Relief Program (TARP), counted 35 such programs with a total federal commitment of $23.7 trillion. As he stated: "I really didn't believe the figure until I saw the backup documents that had been provided by each of the agencies themselves."[6]

Treasury was not a participant in the early cash giveaways. The Department needed Congressional approval, which it got in October 2008, the TARP, $700 billion presumably to be used to buy "toxic mortgages" from banks and generally help homeowners. Instead, the early programs were used to shore up big bank capital. The Fed was able to provide cash to reduce liquidity problems, but not capital to avoid insolvency. The TARP funds invested in bank capital shored up stockholders' equity. By mid-October 2008, Treasury announced preferred stock purchases under TARP to the major banks, including $25 billion to Citigroup and Bank of America, and lesser amounts to J.P. Morgan, Wells Fargo, Goldman Sachs, and other banks.

In the TARP legislation, Congress made clear their interest in protecting homeowners, a position that Treasury and other federal regulators seemed to be uninterested in. Outsiders suggested "cognitive capture," that Treasury and other bureaucrats (beginning with Treasury Secretary Paulson who was previously CEO of Goldman Sachs) had a banking mindset: what was good for the financial community was good public policy. Treasury did announce a number of programs to buy toxic assets from banks. Given little enthusiasm by government officials, none of these programs proved to be successful. Neil Barofsky, former Special Inspector General in Charge of Oversight of TARP, documented Treasury (and other officials) poor performance in *Bailout*.[7] The subtitle tells the tale: "An Inside Account of How Washington Abandoned Main Street While Rescuing Wall Street." In addition, Barofsky's office investigated dozens of fraud cases associated with TARP. By March 2011, 18 people were convicted of TARP-related crimes and many others charged.

The National Bureau of Economic Research (NBER) identified the Great Recession as starting in December 2007 and ending in June 2009. As the unemployment rate was 9.5% in June and topped out at 10% in October, many were skeptical of the NBER pronouncement. However, the economy did slowly recover and Treasury ended most TARP programs by 2010. It was time for Congressional hearings and regulatory action to attempt to stop further abuse.

Regulatory Response

Federal actions were fairly numerous, although slow moving, beginning in 2009. In July of that year President Barack Obama proposed an overhaul of the financial regulatory system, which would add a consumer protection agency and new executive powers. Fed Chairman Bernanke (during Congressional hearings) recommended higher capital requirements, a consolidated regulator of the financial system (preferably the Fed), and more cooperation among regulators. Congressional finance committees held hearings and came up with a huge financial reform bill in 2010. Congress also appointed an inquiry commission on the causes of the crash. The final report was issued after Congress has passed its reform bill. Responses to federal action were mixed, with most analysts critical of its approach, complexity, and failure to regulate certain features such as "too big to fail."

The overhaul plan proposed by President Obama had many components, but was viewed by business as overregulation and by reformers as too modest given the basic financial problems that became obvious with the financial meltdown. It included additional roles for the Federal Reserve (increased capital requirements and new controls on bank holding companies). Also included was the regulation of over-the-counter (OTC) derivatives, resolution authority for the takeover of major financial firms before failure, and the creation of a new Consumer Financial Protection Agency. Some of the president's proposals ended up in the later Dodd-Frank bill.

In July 2009 Congress appointed the Financial Crisis Inquiry Commission to determine the causes of the housing meltdown and recommend corrective actions. The 10-member commission was chaired by Phil Angelides and held its first hearing in September. Six members were appointed by Congressional Democratic leaders and four by Congressional Republicans. Hearings started in January 2010, including heavy hitters such as Goldman Sachs' CEO Lloyd Blankfein, Morgan Stanley CEO John Mack, and J.P. Morgan CEO Jamie Dimon, followed by hundreds of experts in multiple fields. The Commission issued its 500-plus page report in December 2010. The analysis was fairly thorough, but politics played a role in its conclusions. For example, the report concluded that the Community Reinvestment Act, which pushed loan to low income borrowers, was not an important factor. However, Republicans typically consider this a major cause. The final report was approved by six members, while the four members appointed by Republican leaders dissented from the report. Partisanship, of course, makes meaningful legislation difficult.[8]

Congressional hearings were conducted by the House Financial Services Committee chaired by Democrat Barney Frank and the Senate Banking Committee chaired by Democrat Chris Dodd. The bill-writing process proved slow and painful because of substantial disagreement and the perpetual lobbying by the financial industries. The final bill (Dodd-Frank Wall Street Reform and Consumer Protection Act) was passed and signed by the president in July 2010 (months before the Angelides report was issued) to faint praise and severe criticism. It was over 2,200 pages, covered most of the major issues, but seldom to the satisfaction of most reformers. In addition: "the Act requires regulators from at least nine agencies to create 243 new rules, conduct 67 studies, and issue 22 periodic reports."[9] The major criticism was the failure to address the "too big to fail" issue. Opinions were mixed about the potential taxpayer bailouts in future periods. The Act, in 16 titles (sections), is summarized in Table 6.1.

Table 6.1 Wall Street Reform and Consumer Protection (Dodd-Frank) Act Summary

Title I: Financial Stability	Establishes the Financial Stability Oversight Council, chaired by the Treasury Secretary with 10 voting members (the heads of the nine relevant regulators plus an independent member), to settle disputes between federal regulators—with a focus on systemic risk.
Title II: Orderly Liquidation Authority	Expands the list of institutions that can be liquidated; in addition to insured commercial banks now covered by the FDIC and broker-dealers covered by the Securities Investor Protection Corporation (SIPC), the list expands to insurance companies and other financial institutions. An orderly liquidation fund will be capitalized by risk-based assessment fees on "eligible finance companies."
Title III: Transfer of Powers	To streamline bank regulation, the Office of Thrift Supervision is eliminated and its roles transferred to the Federal Reserve, FDIC, and Comptroller of the Currency.
Title IV: Regulation of Advisors to Hedge Funds, Other	Adds substantial regulations and reporting requirement to hedge funds and requires GAO and SEC studies of hedge-fund-related activities.
Title V: Insurance	Established the Federal Insurance Office within the Treasury to monitor the insurance industry and coordinate activities with state insurance regulators.
Title VI: Improvement to Regulations of Banking and Related	Introduces a version of the "Volcker Rule" to limit speculating activities of banks. Banks can own a maximum 3% of equity (defined as "Tier 1 capital")[10] in private equity or hedge funds—and have no direct or indirect relationship with either (except with full disclosure to regulators)
Title VII: Wall Street Transparency and Accountability	Focuses on improved derivative regulation, especially over-the-counter (OTC) swaps and credit derivatives by the Commodity Futures Trading Commission (CFTC) and SEC. Swaps and other OTC derivatives must be cleared through exchanges or clearinghouses to increase transparency in this market.

Title VIII: Payment, Clearing, and Settlement Supervision	Requires the Federal Reserve to develop uniform standards for risk management of "systemically important financial institutions" and increases the Fed's role in supervising risk management related to payment, clearing, and settlement activities associated with trading and other financial transactions.
Title IX: Investor Protections and Improving Securities Regulation	Changes the structure and powers of regulators, including the SEC, credit rating organizations, and broker-dealers or investment advisors. The Office of Investor Advocate is established in the SEC to prevent "regulatory capture" by the SEC. A "whistleblower bounty program" also is established within the SEC. Regulation of credit raters are increased, including an Office of Credit Ratings in the SEC and additional internal control procedures. Additional requirements are placed on the creation and sale of asset-backed securities. Stockholders of public companies get to vote on executive compensation.
Title X: Bureau of Consumer Protection	Establishes the Bureau of Consumer Financial Protection to regulate consumer financial products, with an emphasis on "fair lending." The Bureau obtained enforcement authority in July 2011.
Title XI: Federal Reserve Provisions	Changes somewhat the role of the Fed, including greater oversight starting with audits of the Fed conducted by the GAO and more disclosure. Specific regulatory procedures by the Fed are stated, including establishing capital, risk, liquidity requirements, and off-balance sheet activities.
Title XII: Improving Access	Attempts to improve access and participation of lower-income people (e.g., through pension plans and local governments) of banks ("federally insured depository institutions").
Title XIII: Pay it Back (TARP)	Limits the continued use of Troubled Asset Relief Program (TARP) funding by reducing available funds.
Title XIV: Mortgage Reform and Anti-Predatory Lending	Focuses on the Bureau of Consumer Financial Protection, but aimed specifically at the mortgage market. It required standardized data for mortgage underwriting, mortgage originator requirements, minimum mortgage standards, and various other rules.
Title XV: Miscellaneous	A host of other rules that have little to do with the domestic financial markets, such as IMF requirement, mine safety, and so on.
Title XVI: Section 1256 Contracts	Tax treatment on a variety of derivative instruments.

Several of the provisions are potentially important, depending on specific rules that are written by the agencies involved and actual enforcement. The Bureau of Consumer Financial Protection could be a major force in eliminated predatory practices; however, considerable consumer protection legislation was on the books before the subprime meltdown, but not enforced. Stockholders now vote on executive compensation, potentially the most important factor given the role of incentives in manipulation and fraud. Unfortunately, the votes are not binding and the board of directors can ignore the results. Similar points can be made on new requirements and oversight of derivatives, off-balance-sheet items, and so on. The regulators might be effective or not, depending on the final regulations put into place and actual enforcement. Given all the prior attempts at enforcement of the financial industries, it is hard to be particularly optimistic.

Former Fed Chairman and Obama advisor Paul Volcker proposed the elimination of proprietary trading by banks (that is, trading on their own accounts possibly based on insider information and potentially against the interests of their customers). A watered down version of the Volcker Rule is part of Dodd-Frank. The future effectiveness of Dodd-Frank depends largely on the ultimate regulations written up by the various agencies and the level of actual regulation and enforcement. As stated by bill co-sponsor Chris Dodd, "It will take the next economic crisis, as certainly it will come, to determine whether or not the provisions of this bill will actually provide this generation or the next generation of regulators with the tools necessary to minimize the effects of that crisis."

Accounting Issues: Mark-to-Market, Derivatives, Repo 105s, Special Purpose Entities

Accountants and auditors played supporting roles in the financial debacle of 2008. The professionals did not distinguish themselves by stopping the abuse, but were not leading players as in earlier crises. The most unfortunate point is accountants' involvement were mainly in the same issues as previous failures. Mark-to-market, derivatives, and special purpose entities were major techniques used in the Enron scandals (and many other frauds both before and since). Each played a significant role in the mortgage scandal. All the major financial firms got clean audit opinions annually, despite obvious manipulation, a multitude of suspicious practices, and the oversight of the Public Company Accounting Oversight Board.

Derivatives continued to be a major manipulation issue, despite at least 25 years of substantial problems and scandals beginning with portfolio insurance as the probable cause of the stock market crash in 1987. This was followed by scandals in the 1990s, especially the collapse of Long-term Capital Management (LTCM) and the tech bubble collapse—with Enron particularly prominent. New Financial Accounting Standards Board pronouncements provided more detailed information about derivatives (still a confusing mess to most investors and analysts), but did not resolve important technical issues that are the realm of federal regulators. Particularly problematic are the OTC derivatives where important details were virtually hidden from almost everyone (likely including most buyers). Regulators were unaware of the volume and significance of the OTC products. The growing credit default swaps proved especially dangerous as issuers (AIG in particular) did not consider the substantial risk until the crisis actually hit. Dodd-Frank improves the regulation of OTC derivatives by the Commodities Futures Trading Commission and the SEC, including the use of clearinghouses for OTC transactions.

Special purpose entities became a manipulation symbol with the Enron scandal and the company's use of thousands of SPEs for deceptive purpose and worse. The FASB struggled to account for these flexible entities and now provides guidance (mainly disclosures) through several pronouncements. Because the most obvious purpose of SPEs is to keep liabilities off-balance-sheet, manipulation is often suspected. Banks used SPEs primarily to hold securitized instruments such as MBSs. Citigroup's 2006 10-K (Note 22) showed $2.2 trillion in SPEs (almost $1.5 trillion in MBSs), equivalent to 116% of total assets. At the time Citi had assets to equity of over 18 times (equity of only $120 billion), a substantial amount of leverage; the SPEs were in addition to this. Citi had huge risks in their total portfolio and demonstrated the continued risk associated with SPEs, especially for banks relying on structured finance.

Accounting and Internal Revenue Service (IRS) standards favored historical cost accounting beginning in the late 1930s, in part because of the extreme manipulations associated with fair value accounting. In the post–World War II period fair value was looked on more favorably, with rising inflation being a driving factor. The FASB and SEC instituted increasing use of fair value for financial assets and liabilities, even though manipulation was a problem from the beginning. Once again, Enron was a major proponent of manipulating fair values as were any number of financial institutions. Real estate and structured financial products assumed high valuations, resulting in huge gains reported within the financial industry and expanding compensation of traders, quants, and executives. Complexity proved an important advantage to the perpetrators, as auditors and other investigators typically did not understand the products and could be convinced that generally accepted accounting principles (GAAP) was being followed to the letter.

As mortgage and other securitized markets, as well as real estate, collapsed in 2008, the big financial companies were reluctant to write down collapsing financial products. (Write-offs to fair value in this collapsing market most likely would have wiped out all the equity of the industry.) A major claim was a stable market no longer existed, therefore market prices were unknowable (when prices were booming, the banks made no such claims). Auditors and regulators did not seem to challenge any of these claims. An accommodating FASB issued Staff Position 157-4 in April, 2009, agreeing with this position and eliminated the requirement that securitized products be written down to fair value because of disrupted markets. The financial firms no longer had an urgent need to write down or sell toxic assets and likely maintained them on the books for years. This was a substantial factor in banking stability, but makes observers question the merits of fair value accounting. Pundits made the case that the banks pocket the profits, but taxpayers pay the losses. To that can be added: banks book fair value profits, but not necessarily fair value losses.

During the 21st century, auditors did uncover accounting abuses and fraud of various financial companies, in part because of Sarbanes-Oxley requirements. Internal control reports for AIG and General Electric noted control weaknesses associated with financial products. Fannie Mae, Freddie Mac, and AIG had additional accounting problems before the financial crisis. AIG was a giant well-regulated insurance company, except for its entrance into credit default swaps. AIG held over half a trillion dollars worth of CDSs before the crash and therefore the company faced huge liabilities and likely failure.

Accounting irregularities were common at Fannie and Freddie. Both expanded their mortgage portfolios relying on extreme leverage to meet earnings growth targets (providing executives huge compensation packages) plus unreported derivative use and accounting fraud. When Freddie replaced Arthur Andersen after the Enron scandal with Pricewaterhouse-Coopers, the new auditor found manipulation over several years and forced Freddie to restate earnings by $5 billion. Irregularities also were found by Deloitte & Touche at Fannie. The SEC forced some $6 billion of earnings restatements in 2004, related to about a dozen accounting violations. Although the CEOs were fired, manipulation did not end. After extreme losses in 2007–2008, both companies had negative equity (i.e., insolvency—a standard definition of failure) and were forced into federal conservatorship.

Investment banks and other financial institutions relied on repurchase agreements for short-term financing (cash is exchanged for financial assets serving as collateral, often overnight; the borrower reverses the entry the next day). A repo 105 has 105% collateral and actually books the "loan" as a "sale"; consequently, on the books cash replaces the financial assets used as collateral and liabilities are not recognized. This was accepted as GAAP and caused little stir until after the failure of Lehman Brothers when the bankruptcy court examiner exposed the scam. This was certainly manipulation, but because it was allowed by GAAP it was not fraud—although New York Attorney General Andrew Cuomo charged: "Lehman engaged in a massive accounting fraud." Cuomo filed charges against Lehman's auditor, Ernst & Young, for aiding the bank in this alleged fraud. The FASB changed the accounting requirements for repos in 2011.

Lessons to be Learned

The financial meltdown of 2008 was a financial rather than an accounting crisis, but accountants played a supporting role and the results were disastrous—the first crash calculated in the trillions of dollars. Major reasons included incentives run amuck, extreme deregulation, and financial innovations not understood by investors, executives, or regulators. Accounting issues were similar to the previous tech meltdown at the turn of the century: SPEs, derivatives, and mark-to-market. Once again, a massive reform bill resulted with experts and pundits debating its future effectiveness. Unfortunately, the economic and financial world is too complex and dynamic with robust incentives to cheat and regulations difficult to enforce. The incentives of executives, board members, politicians, auditors, and regulators are not much different than before the last crash. Regulators often have limited expertise and perhaps incentives not to be particularly diligent (e.g., given the potential for future high-paying jobs in the industry being regulated). Politicians still want to be reelected and seem to find big political contributions irresistible.

All is not entirely lost. Many if not most regulators, for example, are hard-working and reasonably effective. Most executives do a stellar job, as do auditors and the various other players. Business culture in the future may favor greater ethical behavior and a longer view of performance. There will always be cheaters and big-time fraudsters; perhaps the built-in oversight will spot them before they can do too much damage. Clearing houses now exist for other-the-counter derivatives; stockholders vote on executive compensation; financial reports must be filed quickly. A related key is reducing information asymmetries. Manipulation is much more difficult if all the players have the necessary information for decision-making.

CHAPTER 7

The Future of Fraud and Scandals

A boom without crooks is like a dog without fleas. … Why do periods of great prosperity always wind up being periods of great scandals? It's not that it happens occasionally. It happens every time. The railroad boom makes the Internet boom look clean. … Is it possible that scandal is somehow an essential ingredient in capitalism? That a healthy free-market economy must tempt a certain number of people to behave corruptly, and that a certain number of these will do so? That the crooks are not a sign that something is rotten but that something is working more or less as it was meant to work?

—Michael Lewis

Manipulation and scandals are well established and, despite the best efforts of standard setters, regulators, and auditors, expected to have a continuing future. Points one is motivation. When the incentives exist to cheat, a substantial percent of people are expected to cheat. Almost from the beginning, America was about capitalism and free markets,[1] relying on entrepreneurial innovations, but simultaneously with short-term corruption. Government action could be ambiguous, from generous support, to apathy, to seeming antipathy for economic progress. The roles of innovation, entrepreneurship, and corruption are complex. Corruption could be hard to resist even by wealthy and successful businesspeople—private gain provides opportunities for corruption and exploitation. As long as incentives exist, expect corruption to continue.

Key Points on Continuing Scandals

Types of fraud and corruption changed over time, from smuggling and bribery, to land speculation, political machines, and bank frauds, to massive corporations using conspiracies and monopoly power, to mass-market speculation, stock pyramiding, and price manipulation, to widespread earnings manipulation and growing accounting fraud, to manipulation and speculation with innovative financial innovations in derivatives and structured finance. Accounting seems to have played an increasing role over time, largely because of the importance of accounting standards, formal financial disclosures, and required audits. Accountants seemed necessary for the conspiracies to work and other accountants needed to uncover the fraud.

The Progressive Movement of the late 19th century, combined with muckraking journalists and activist politicians led to federal regulations, from the Sherman Act of 1890 though reforms under Woodrow Wilson. However, major changes to the perspective of federal responsibilities came with Franklin Roosevelt's New Deal. Those regulations and enforcement (including the Securities and Exchange Commission (SEC) and substantial changes in banking) proved reasonably effective for half a century. Manipulation and fraud certainly occurred (as has bribery for the last 10,000 years), but enforcement seemed to work reasonably well.

Beginning in the 1970s increased inflation, global competition, energy problems, and so on created economic cracks. The banking system provided new services and got exponentially bigger, a deregulation mindset led to lax enforcement, combined with increased speculation and manipulation. Tax cuts, ironically, and other changes resulted in greater interest in compensation especially at the top of big organizations. The incentives were in place for new boom-bust cycles. The last two, the tech bubble and subprime collapse, have been particularly severe. The misaligned incentive structures are obvious and many recommendations have been made about needed institutional changes, from the Volcker Rule to "too-big-to-fail" solutions, political fixes, corporate governance, and executive compensation reforms.

Accounting and Auditing Issues

Various problematic accounting issues refuse to go away, dealing with complex instruments and contracts difficult to account for and allow for continued manipulation.

These include the major issues from Enron and the Subprime Meltdown: derivatives, mark-to-market, and special purpose entities. Other continuing issues include pension and other retirement benefits, acquisition accounting, taxes (including off-shore operations), and executive compensation. There involve long-term contracts, financial markets, and government regulations. The accounting role is how to properly book transactions and how complex information should be disclosed. The auditing role is discussed below. Generally, accounting procedures and disclosures have improved for these items. This should limit information asymmetries, potentially reducing but not eliminating the potential for manipulation and fraud.

Auditors have a major role in minimizing aggressive accounting. Although external auditors are paid by the companies being audited, they are on the front line of monitoring and have regulatory obligations to ensure that abuse and fraud are nonexistent. Accounting researchers have considerable evidence on what constitutes high-quality audits, using empirical surrogates to describe theoretical and professional relationships.

According to Christensen et al.,[2] "audit professionals most frequently define a high quality audit as one performed and documented in accordance with generally accepted auditing standards (GAAS) to provide reasonable assurance that financial statements are not materially misstated." Some of the common measures of poor quality audits are the existence of earnings restatements (from previous years that almost always had unqualified opinions in those earlier years), SEC comment letters and enforcement actions, and reports of deficiencies by the Public Company Accounting Oversight Board. Other potential signals of poor audit quality include very low audit fees, small audit firms (rather than the Big Four and other "second tier" auditors such as Grant Thornton or BDO Seidman), and technical measures of discretionary accruals used by researchers (a greater magnitude of accruals suggest more manipulation).

Expected Outcomes: What Are the Incentives?

"Follow the money." That was Deep Throat's advice to journalist Bob Woodward uncovering the Watergate scandal in the 1970s. The same advice applies to finance and accounting scandals. Consequently, many of the same types of fraud from the past will recur because incentives are fundamentally unchanged, while regulations and enforcement to eliminate potential scandals remain questionable. Most of these are the same troublemakers from Enron and the various 1990s financial scandals: excessive and badly designed executive compensation contracts, mark-to-market, and that trifecta of financial abuse: structured finance, special purpose entities, and derivatives. Scandals emanating from the financial sector are particularly likely because of their substantial incentives and long history of manipulation. Add to that the likely "cognitive capture" of the Treasury Department and other regulators and the odds of continuing scandals seem high.

Accounting will likely play only a supporting role, given the continuing institutional framework. Auditors are still agent for (and paid by) corporations and have never shown a propensity to discover fraud. The previously mentioned trifecta of financial abuse are subject to greater disclosure requirements, but these accounting rules are not likely to deter future fraud. Major subprime player Citigroup disclosed their trifecta extremely well, for example, without setting off major alarm bells.[3]

Although the underlying incentives seem roughly the same, the institutional environment—especially regulatory reform—has been modified. Consequently, the when, where, and how of specific scandals are hard to determine. Just as hackers perpetually attack the Pentagon, the fraudsters probe for institutional weaknesses. The big players have high-powered talent and past experience demonstrates their effectiveness.

Businesses seriously promoting social responsibility (i.e., acting in the best interests of all stakeholders including the general public) are unlikely to promote illicit practices, but relatively few corporations seem particularly serious about social responsibility—remember the economics of bad behavior. Businesspeople, on the other hand, interested only in maximizing short-term stockholder wealth and executive compensation (and perhaps only interested in the executive compensation part) are certainly continuing candidates for manipulation and fraud.

Timeline

Accounting Scandals and Reform

Scandal	Period	Discussion
Smuggling and Bribery	From the beginning	Smuggling and bribery have been common practices since the earliest civilizations and from the start of the North American colonies. As restrictions became increasingly tight, smuggling and bribery became more sophisticated.
Counterfeiting	Shortly after the invention of money	Counterfeiting also has ancient origins. In colonial and early American periods, counterfeiting paper money became prevalent and boomed as state bank charters exploded in the 19th century.
American Constitution	Written in 1787	Unable to function adequately under the Articles of Confederation, a new constitution was debated, written, and passed; despite immense problems (especially slavery), the federal system proved effective.
Panic of 1792	1792	William Duer tried to use his insider information to corner the New York bank stock; he failed, went bankrupt, and the market panicked. As Treasury Secretary, Alexander Hamilton flooded the economy with cash and limited the economic damage.
Yazoo Land Scandal	1795	Georgia politicians and speculators sold raw land in what became Mississippi, despite lack of legal ownership.
Speculative Banking	From early 19th century	Each state established a banking experiment, from conservative and long-lasting to wildcat banking, resulting in massive speculation, fraud, and counterfeiting of bank notes.
Political Machines	From early 19th century	New York City's Democratic machine, Tammany Hall, became a long-term source of power and corruption, and was emulated by American local and state governments throughout the nation.
Stock Market Manipulation	From early 19th century	Stock markets were established for their members benefit and these and other masters of manipulation made (and occasionally lost) fortunes to the detriment of investors (aka, dumb money).
Civil War Legislation	1861–1865	Union financing required substantial new tax laws and an updated banking system regulated by the Treasury Department.

Accounting Scandals and Reform (Continued)

Scandal	Period	Discussion
Credit Mobilier	1862–1872	Federal legislation during the Civil War chartered and financed the first transcontinental railroad, constructed by the Union Pacific and Central Pacific railroads. Both railroads used separate construction companies to siphon off millions of dollars to the promoters. Congressional hearings discovered the massive fraud at Credit Mobilier, the construction company created to finance the Union Pacific construction.
Raiding the Erie	1868	Cornelius Vanderbilt went after the Erie Railroad to complete his dominance of New York transportation and end the corruption done by Daniel Drew and other Erie manipulators. Drew and confederates Jay Gould and Jim Fisk fought back, in part by issuing new shares of Erie and both sides used judges and the New York legislature to get their way "legally." Vanderbilt eventually gave up.
Cornering Gold	1869	Jay Gould and Jim Fisk attempted to corner the New York gold market when most of the gold stock was shipped west to pay for harvested agricultural goods. President U.S. Grant stopped the scam by releasing gold from the federal stockpile.
William ("Boss") Tweed	Post–Civil War	Tweed ran Tammany Hall; the level of corruption was so vast he and his "Ring" were prosecuted and Tween died in jail. His downfall can be attributed, in part, to famous Thomas Nast cartoons.
Corporate Conspiracy and Merger Movement	1860s to early 20th century	Corporations created by John D. Rockefeller in oil, Andrew Carnegie in steel, several railroad trusts, and hundreds more established huge national and multinational empires despite archaic government regulations, using newly invented trusts, various price conspiracies, and more flexible state incorporation laws. The New York "Money Trust" established massive corporate giants with monopoly power in dozens of industries, culminating in U.S. Steel in 1901, America's first billion-dollar enterprise.
Sherman Antitrust Act	1890	The federal government regulated railroads with the Interstate Commerce Commission Act of 1887 and began antitrust enforcement with the Sherman Act. Government wins included the breakup of the Northern Pacific Railroad and Rockefeller's Standard Oil.

Accounting Scandals and Reform (Continued)

Scandal	Period	Discussion
CPA Licensing	From 1896	New York was the first state to license auditors as "certified public accountants," based on experience and written exam results. All other states would eventually follow.
Panic of 1907	1907	Speculation to corner United Copper, the failure of trust companies and brokers led to the panic and depression. Investigations and Pujo Committee hearings followed.
Pujo Committee Hearings	1913	Congressional hearings on the "Money Trust" documented many of the illicit activities of Money Trust banks and Wall Street. Reform legislation followed.
Sixteenth Amendment. Federal Reserve, Federal Trade Commission, Clayton Act	1913–1914	Substantial federal reform legislation followed the Pujo Hearings, including new anti-trust and related legislation, the creation of the Federal Reserve System and Federal Trade Commission, and a permanent federal income tax.
Charles Ponzi	1920	Ponzi developed his eponymous scheme looking for greedy but gullible investors wanting to make a fortune in International Reply Coupons. He promised a 50% return in 45 days and paid off early "investors" to entice more. He was shut down within a few months after collecting millions and sent to prison before being deported back to Italy.
Teapot Dome	1920s	The presidency of Warren G. Harding was essentially "bought" by oil interests. During the Harding presidency, the Interior Department leased Teapot Dome and other oil properties to oilmen for bribes to Interior Secretary Albert Fall. When discovered, the leases were cancelled and Fall jailed for bribery.
Stock Maneuvering and Speculation	1920s	It was anything goes at the New York Stock Exchange, including insider trading, stock pools for price manipulation, and stock pyramiding. Stock prices fueled by speculation and margin buying created a bubble that collapsed at the end of 1929, ultimately resulting in the Great Depression of the 1930s.
Ultramares Case	1924	Auditor Touche Niven gave a company an unqualified opinion although substantial fraud was present. Ultramares, the lender, sued to auditor. The court found Touche negligent but not fraudulent and therefore not liable.

Accounting Scandals and Reform (Continued)

Scandal	Period	Discussion
Krueger and Toll	1920s and 1930s	Ivar Krueger established a financial empire created on matches and fraud. The company did not disclose finances but paid consistent dividends from cash on new securities sold. After the complete collapse of his firm, he killed himself before the full extent of his fraud was uncovered.
Insull Utility Bankruptcy	1931	Samuel Insull built an electric utility empire based on leverage, a process called stock pyramiding. Much of the profits came from writing up utility assets to "fair value." With little equity, the corporation collapsed early in the Great Depression.
Pecora Commission	1932–1934	Congressional hearings on the causes of the market crash and Great Depression, documenting the abusive practices of business and Wall Street. New Deal Legislation followed.
Securities Acts	1933–1934	Based on the findings of massive wrongdoing on Wall Street and at corporations, the Securities Acts under FDR's New Deal created the SEC to regulate securities markets and provide adequate disclosures of public corporations' finances.
McKesson & Robbins	1937	Massive fraud scheme by the president of this pharmaceutical company, including nonexistent inventory and receivables. Fraud continued for years because auditor Price Waterhouse did not audit either. Audit regulation was demanded. The Committee on Audit Procedures was established in 1939 to issue auditing standards, beginning with requirements to physically conduct inventory and confirm receivables.
Creation of Committee on Accounting Procedures	1938	CAP created to established generally accepted accounting principles (GAAP), using Accounting Research Bulletins. Fifty-one ARBs were issued over 20 years (1938–59). These represented many of the fundamental accounting standards still in use (although the particulars have changed over time).
Accounting Principles Board	1959	The ABP replaced the CAP, using new procedures but with many of problems of the previous organization.
Investor Overseas Services	1960s	IOS, headquartered in Switzerland, was a mutual fund fraud conducted by back-to-back CEOs Bernie Cornfeld and Robert Vesco, both spending time in jail.

Accounting Scandals and Reform (Continued)

Scandal	Period	Discussion
Great Salad Oil Swindle	1963	Allied Crude Vegetable Oil filled tankers with water and topped off with salad oil. Inspectors for creditors confirmed shipments of salad oil. Creditors lost millions and CEO Tino De Angelis spent seven years in jail.
Continental Vending	1969	A criminal case against the auditors of Continental Vending where Lybrand Ross certified financial statement known to be false. Although Lybrand did not violate GAAS, three Lybrand auditors were found guilty of criminal fraud.
Equity Funding	1972	This small insurance company issued fraudulent financial statements to stay afloat; closed by SEC based on whistle-blower disclosures.
Financial Accounting Standards Board	1973	The FASB was established to replace the APB, with an improved process, governance, and public involvement.
National Student Marketing	1975	Provided jobs to college students and other services that proved to be bogus. Founder Cortes Randell convicted of stock fraud.
Foreign Corrupt Practices Act	1977	After several bribery scandals of foreign officials, this Act made bribery in foreign countries for business purposes illegal. It also mandated internal control requirements of public firms.
Advertising Ban Eliminated on Auditors	1979	Prompted by federal pressure, the ban on advertising by audit firms was lifted. An unintended consequence was "lowballing," a very low bid to get a new client. During the 1980s and beyond, the audit was more and more priced as a commodity—possibly resulting in lower quality audits.
Deregulation of the Savings & Loan Industry	1982	Garn-St. Germain Act deregulated S&Ls because of the problems caused by rising interest rates. The deregulations helped avoid immediate bankruptcy of much of the industry, but created a soon-to-be corrupt industry that required a federal bailout. Much of the industry would fail and dozens of executives jailed.
Michael Milken	1980s	Milken specialized in making a market in junk bonds, but multiplied his wealth by manipulating price data, insider trading, illegal outside deals, tax fraud, and other elements of a vast criminal conspiracy. His downfall also forced Drexel Burnham into bankruptcy.

Accounting Scandals and Reform (Continued)

Scandal	Period	Discussion
EMS Government Securities	1986	Securities firm hid speculative losses through fraud and bribed the outside auditor, a CPA, to cover up the fraud. Several of the perpetrators received long jail terms, although the CPA only got a modest sanction by the state board.
ZZZZ Best	1986	Small insurance restoration company becoming successful based on increasing levels of fraud by founder Barry Minkow, who was jailed in 1989.
BCCI Scandal	1988	This Middle Eastern bank had a criminal structure to launder money, facilitate the drug trade and arms trafficking, evade taxes, and use politicians to buy influence. Criminal indictments stated in 1988, which led to the bank's failure in the early 1990s.
Savings & Loan (S&L) Bailout	1989 to early 1990s	S&L crisis with substantial fraud resulted in the failure of over 700 S&Ls, which were closed by the Regulation Trust Corporation (RTC). The RTC sold billions of dollars of S&L assets, resulting in a net loss to taxpayers of almost $100 billion.
Public Securities Litigation Reform Act	1995	This accountant-friendly legislation reduced the potential legal liabilities of external auditors, leading to the potential for more aggressive audits—which seemed to be the result in the late 1990s and beyond.
Waste Management	1997	This trash, waste, and landfill business was a good metaphor for the underlying accounting, which included overstated revenues and understated expenses—with a focus on fraudulent accounting for property, plant, and equipment. The firm failed after earnings restatements of over $1 billion for a five-year period.
Sunbeam	1998	A failing appliance manufacturer hired Al Dunlap to turn the company around; costs were cut, profits rose, but were maintained only by fraudulent revenue recognition and other illegal acts. Sunbeam was forced to write off over $1 billion from previous years before declaring bankruptcy.
Cendant	1998	The conglomerate HFS increased profits through acquisitions. However, the company acquired CUC International (and changed its name to Cendant). Unfortunately, CUC used fraudulent accounting for years, which was uncovered only after the acquisition was completed.

Accounting Scandals and Reform (Continued)

Scandal	Period	Discussion
Long-term Capital Management	1998	This giant hedge fund, reputed to be run by the smarted financial experts, used overextended leverage and was on the wrong side of trillion dollar bets on the Russian ruble and other ill-advised hedging. It took a Federal Reserve–backed bailout to clear the exposed positions and protect the financial world.
Rite Aid	1999	This drugstore chain had several accounting issues, which led to earnings restatements, SEC, and other investigations and lawsuits. Executives were fired and jailed.
Regulation FD (Full Disclosure)	2001	SEC required increased public disclosure when companies talked to analysts and other investment insiders. Earnings announcements were required to be made public, usually through Internet simulcasts.
Enron	2001	Enron transformed from a stogy gas pipeline company to a gas trader that claimed to be a global high-tech company. This facade was maintained through fraud, including the widespread use of special purpose entities, derivatives, and deceptive use of trading profits. Possibly the biggest business scandal in American history, several executives were jailed.
WorldCom	2002	Large telecom company temporarily avoided failure when actual profits collapsed by simple fraud: recorded operating expenses as capital assets—some $11 billion. Several executives were jailed including CEO Bernie Ebbers.
Adelphia	2002	Cable TV empire used accounting fraud in part to compensate for corporate governance violations to benefit Regas family members. Adelphia went bankrupt and several Regas's employees (all on the board) went to jail.
Tyco	2002	Large conglomerate using typical aggressive merger accounting practices to increase earnings plus other illicit practices. Company forced to restate earnings, and paid fines to settle SEC charges and class-action lawsuits. CEO Dennis Kozlowski and others sent to prison.
Imclone	2002	Biopharmaceutical company whose executives were charged with insider trading for dumping stock before bad news disclosed to the public. CEO Samuel Waksal also notified Martha Stewart to sell. Both Waksal and Stewart ended up in prison.

Accounting Scandals and Reform (Continued)

Scandal	Period	Discussion
Sarbanes-Oxley Act	2002	After the Enron and WorldCom scandals and all the rest, Congress passed financial reform, including new rules on corporate governance, internal control, auditing, and the creation of the Public Company Accounting Oversight Board.
HealthSouth	2003	Operating inpatient rehabilitation facilities and became the first post-Sarbanes-Oxley scandal. Profits were maintained by aggressive merger accounting, overcharging Medicare, and other fraud techniques. The company restated earnings for $2.5 billion in 2002 and declared bankruptcy in 2003.
Fannie Mae	2004	Fannie Mae and, to a lesser extent, Freddie Mac, were repeat violators of accounting and manipulators of other rules, including ignoring derivative losses. Fannie was forced to restate over $6 billion in earnings in 2004 by the SEC. Both Fannie and Freddie would be placed into federal conservatorship in 2008.
AIG	2005	Giant insurance company and part of the Dow Jones Industrial Average was cited for substantial internal control weaknesses and SEC fraud investigation led to a $1.6 billion fine and criminal charges filed against several executives.
Stock Option Backdating	2006	The SEC discovered that dozens of companies were backdating stock option awards to increase executive compensation. Several executives were prosecuted. A number of other stock options manipulations were uncovered including exercise backdating, spring-loading, and speed vesting.
Sub-prime Loan Scandal	2007–2008	Mortgage lending became a massive manipulation scheme involving predatory lending practices, structured finance of mortgages manipulated to appear high quality, and widespread speculation. The scandals started to unravel in 2007 as housing prices declined.
Bear Stearns Failure	2008	Fed and Treasury bailed out a failing Bear Stearns, which had no liquidity to meet its obligations in March 2008; Bear was acquired by J.P. Morgan after the feds agreed to be responsible for up to $30 billion in toxic assets.

Accounting Scandals and Reform (Continued)

Scandal	Period	Discussion
Conservatorship of Fannie and Freddie	2008	In the summer of 2008, the feds took over the failing GSEs, which had lost billion, had negative equity, and maintained trillions of dollars of mortgage securities and guarantees.
Failure of Lehman Brothers	2008	Following Bear Stearns, Lehman Brothers was allowed to fail in October, the nation's largest bankruptcy. The reaction was almost a complete paralysis of the global credit markets, requiring multitrillion dollar liquidity packages by the Federal Reserve and the creation of the Troubled Asset Relief Program (TARP).
Bailout of AIG	2008	After the Lehman failure, the feds bailed out AIG by providing $180 billion in equity to avoid the failure of the world's largest insurance company.
TARP	2008	After Treasury and Fed prodding, Congress passed the Troubled Asset Relief Program (TARP) that provided billions of dollars of capital to failing banks. The bill was originally designed to bail out mortgage holders, which happened only to a limited extent.
Bernard Madoff	2008	Madoff was a NASDAQ innovator and trader who created a multibillion dollar Ponzi scheme that lasted for decades. When the investor cash ran out in 2008, he confessed to fraud and theft and was sentenced to 150 years in jail.
Goldman Sachs	2010	The SEC filed a fraud lawsuit against Goldman in the Abacus 2007-AC1 case, a collateralized debt obligation structured finance deal gone bad, losing millions of dollars of investor money. Goldman settled, paying a $550 million fine to the SEC and investors.
Dodd-Frank Act	2010	Congress eventually passed the massive Financial Reform bill in 2010 "to promote the financial stability of the United States by improving accountability and transparency in the financial system, to end 'too big to fail,' to protect the American taxpayer by ending bailouts, to protect consumers from abusive financial services practices, and for other purposes." The potential effectiveness has been debated ever since.
Raj Rajaratnam	2011	Rajaratnam, head of hedge fund Galleon Group, convicted of insider training, one of several financial insiders indicted and convicted.

Accounting Scandals and Reform (Continued)

Scandal	Period	Discussion
LIBOR Scandal	2012	The London Interbank Offered Rate (LIBOR), a short-term interest rate (trillions of dollars of derivatives are priced based on LIBOR), was manipulated by major London banks for their own benefit. The story was broken by the *Financial Times* in July 2012.
London Whale	2012	Huge trading losses (over $6 billion) by Bruno Iksil (the "London Whale") at J.P. Morgan's London branch based on derivative transactions.
Internal Revenue Scandal	2013	IRS targeted conservative groups applying for tax-exempt status for extra scrutiny, resulting in investigations by the FBI and Attorney General.
SAC Capital Indictment	2013	Hedge fund SAC Capital charged by Justice Department with a "culture of insider trading" by encouraging traders to tap personal contacts about public companies; charges based in part on wire taps and e-mails.

Notes

Chapter 1

1. Hermanson et al. (1993), p. 3.
2. According to Giroux (2013, pp. 234–235), fraud involves four characteristics: a false statement or representation, knowledge that it is false, reliance by the person receiving the statement, and financial damages caused by the false statement. The Federal Bureau of Investigation's (FBI) list of common fraud schemes includes telemarketing, identity theft, healthcare fraud, Ponzi schemes, pyramid schemes, non-delivery of merchandise, and counterfeiting (currency, drugs, etc.).
3. Gordon (2004), p. 207.
4. The most corruption-free cultures are Denmark, Finland, and New Zealand. See the Transparency International webpage (www.transparency.org) for the complete list and considerable information about corruption around the world. According to Google, the term "culture of corruption" first appeared in the 1950s and its use exploded in the last 30 years.
5. Freeland (2012), pp. 223–225.
6. Giroux (2004), pp. 2–4.
7. Frank (2012), p. 39.
8. Schilit (2002), p. 28.
9. Regulatory capture is an economic theory that the responsible agency works to benefit the regulated industry rather than the public interest—the reason they were created. That seemed to develop in the railroad industry, regulated by the Interstate Commerce Commission from 1887. Most recently, the Treasury Department and Federal Reserve seemed more interested in protecting banks than bank customers burned in the subprime meltdown. A more recent explanation from psychology is cognitive capture, in this case regulators having the same perceptions as the executives of the regulated industry. Hank Paulson was CEO of Goldman Sachs before becoming Treasury Secretary (with many senior regulatory executives with similar backgrounds). His reactions to crisis protected banks, but it is less clear if the public benefitted.
10. It is difficult to put Greenspan at the top of the villains' list, given the arguably incompetent CEOs collecting hundreds of millions of dollars in compensation based on short-sighted greed that destroyed their companies and almost brought down world finances. Richard Fuld of Lehman Brothers

and Jimmy Cayne of Bear Stearns come to mind (numbers one and three, respectively, on *Portfolio's* list of worst CEOs ever).

11. Johnston (2012), pp. 77–89.
12. Johnston (2012), p. 82.
13. Giroux (2004).
14. Friedman (1970).
15. Friedman (1970), p. 3.
16. Rosenberg (2012), p. 81.
17. Strine (2012).
18. Strine (2012), p. 2.
19. Strine (2012), p. 2.
20. Strine (2012), p. 3.
21. Strine (2012), p. 3.
22. Strine (2012), p. 1.

Chapter 2

1. *Smuggler Nation* by Peter Andreas (2013) looks at the long history of smuggling in the United States, which started early, was pervasive and much more widespread than generally believed and continued in various forms throughout America's entire history. Several founding fathers, including John Hancock, were major smugglers.

2. Chandler's *The Visible Hand: The Managerial Revolution in American Business* (1977), winner of the Pulitzer Prize, brilliantly examines the rise of business beginning about 1790 in considerable detail. Although the book focuses on professional management including the importance of accounting, little emphasis is placed on corruption or fraud. Despite that, this book is the best historical overview of the importance of professional management.

3. Chandler (1977), p. 109.
4. Josephson (1934), p. 133.
5. Ambrose (2000), p. 320.
6. Livesay (2000), p. 29.
7. Chandler (1977), p. 109.
8. Chandler (1977), p. 179.
9. Brunnermeier and Oehmke (2012).
10. Gladwell (2005), p. 76 described the Warren Harding error thus: "Many people who looked at Warren Harding saw how extraordinarily handsome and distinguished-looking he was and jumped to the immediate—and entirely unwarranted—conclusion that he was a man of courage and intelligence and integrity. ... The Warren Harding error is the dark side of rapid

cognition. It is at the root of a good deal of prejudice and discrimination. It's why picking the right candidate for a job is so difficult and why, on more occasions than we may care to admit, utter mediocrities sometimes end up in positions of enormous responsibility."

Chapter 3

1. Chernow (1990), p. 351.
2. Chernow (1990), p. 355.
3. MacLeish (1933).
4. MacLeish (1933).
5. Investment Trusts (1929).
6. Seligman (2003), p. 66.
7. Hawkins (1986), p. 380.
8. Giroux (1996), p. 28.
9. A similar case occurred in the previous decade. Touche Niven (now Deloitte and Touche, a Big Four auditor) gave Fred Stern and Company an unqualified opinion in 1924. Like McKesson, Stern also falsified inventory and receivables, which were not audited by Touche. Stern's lender, Ultramares Corp., sued Touche to recover the loan amount after Stern failed. The court found Touche negligent but not fraudulent (and therefore not liable), a victory for Touche but not for appropriate auditing procedures.

Chapter 4

1. Geisst (2000), p. 224.
2. Gladwell (2008), pp. 124–127.
3. Private equity firms (PEFs) are investment firms investing in companies using a variety of strategies (friendly or hostile takeovers, LBOs, venture—or vulture—capital). Like hedge funds, PEFs have a limited number of investors to avoid SEC regulations. Starting in the late 1940s, PEFs first boomed in the 1980s using LBOs and junk bond financing.
4. Stewart (1991), p. 219.
5. Small (immaterial) frauds at big companies (such as stealing inventory or cash or even embezzlement) are typically ignored in corporate reports. Thousands of such cases probably occur annually.
6. Noah (2001).
7. Government Accountability Office (2002).
8. Schilit (2002).
9. Zeff (2003a), pp. 189–205.

10. Cassell and Giroux (2011), pp. 177–183.

11. Cassell and Giroux (2011), pp. 180–182.

Chapter 5

1. King (2006), p. 162.

2. My personal favorite book on Enron is Kurt Eichenwald's *Conspiracy of Fools*. It is longer than the rest and came out only in 2005; consequently, it has additional content as new information was made available. Other interesting books include Mimi Swartz and Sherron Watkins's *Power Failure: The Insider Story of the Collapse of Enron*. Watkins, a vice president at Enron, was the insider. Also of interest is Bethany McLean and Peter Elkind's *The Smartest Guys in the Room*. McLean and Elkind were journalists following the story for *Fortune*.

3. Profits on long-term contracts using historical cost are recorded over the life of the contract, roughly matching cash flows. All the expected gain can be recognized immediately using fair value. However, the long-term contract must be revalued every period, with the potential for either gains or losses as fair value changes. The unanswered question is which method provides the best measure of performance.

4. Rich Kinder started a new stogy pipeline company with William Morgan, becoming CEO. Kinder Morgan had a market value in 2013 of $36 billion and Kinder is a multi-billionaire. Apparently, a case can be made for slow, conservative growth free of complex manipulation.

5. McLean and Elkind (2002), p. 155.

6. When using the equity method, based on ownership of about 20–50% of a subsidiary, only the net amount (share of assets less liabilities) is reported as a long-term investment. Thus, it eliminates consolidating the liabilities (and assets) of the subsidiary. Joint ventures are usually 50–50 partnerships by two owners, each recording their share using the equity method.

7. Toffler (2003), pp. 62–63.

8. Missing the 60-day deadline is considered a significant event and usually requires a separate 8-K report and a Notification of Late filing on Form 12b–25 to the SEC, stating the reason(s) for the delay. This can be considered a red flag by financial analysts.

9. Cassell et al. (2012).

10. Giroux (2006).

11. Murphy (2012), pp. 92–93.

12. High-frequency traders now use robot trading to front-run large investors buying and selling on the NYSE and other exchanges, a new high-tech

illicit practice increasing the cost of basic market transactions. See Scott Patterson's *Dark Pools* (2012) for a more detailed analysis.

Chapter 6

1. McLean and Nocera (2010), p. 111.
2. After losing billions of dollars, both Fannie and Freddie became profitable beginning in 2012, in part based on tax-loss carry-forwards (which will continue for years). See Shawn Tully's article in *Fortune* (2013).
3. Wessel (2009), p. 17.
4. A CDS pays off if the underlying debt instrument defaults. Designed to allow a creditor to hedge against default by paying a premium to the third party (an insurance company, for example), it remained an unregulated market. Naked CDSs were allowed, meaning buyers (basically speculators) did not have to own the underlying debt. The majority of the market (estimated at 80%) became naked CDSs. In addition, sellers often did not hold reserves against potential payouts.
5. Wessell (2009), pp. 173–174.
6. Barofsky (2012), p.162.
7. Barofsky (2012).
8. A common stalling tactic is to establish a task force or commission to spend months on a difficult issue (with as many pro-lobby group members as possible) and then fail to agree on a solution. Often the regulatory topic no longer seems urgent.
9. Murphy (2012), p. 111.
10. The Basel Committee on Banking Supervision (made up primarily of central bankers from major countries) in Switzerland created the Basel Accords, which focused on capital requirements. Banks are required to hold equity equal to 8% of their risk-weighted assets. Credit risk is divided into five classes, with Tier 1 capital presumed riskless (investments in Treasury securities and other sovereign debt, for example). The greater the risk, the more equity has to be held.

Chapter 7

1. It can be argued that smuggling within the colonies created a relatively free market within a highly regulated mercantilist system. The ethics of smuggling can be debated, but America had plenty of big-time smugglers.
2. Christensen et al. (2013), p. 3.

3. Anyone willing to slog through the notes of the Citi 2006 10-K would discover the previously noted securitization through special purpose entities (called special purpose vehicles) of $2.2 trillion laid out in an informative table by category. In addition, Citi also included a table on derivatives, totaling $29.3 trillion with almost $2 trillion in "credit derivatives" (mainly CDSs). In other words, the astronomical amounts that later shocked the regulators (and just amount everyone else) were in plain sight.

Bibliography

Adams, C., & Henry, A. (1871). *Chapters of Erie and other essays.* Boston, MA: James A. Osgood.

Ahamed, L. (2009). *Lords of finance: The bankers who broke the world.* New York, NY: Penguin Books.

Akerlof, G., & Paul, R. (1993). Looting: The economic underworld of bankruptcy for profit. *Brookings Papers on Economic Activity 24*(2), 1–73.

Akerlof, G., & Robert, S. (2009). *Animal spirits: How human psychology drives the economy, and why it matters for global capitalism.* Princeton, NJ: Princeton University Press.

(1929). *Business: Allegheny Corp.* Retrieved February 11, 1929, from Time: www.time.com

Ambrose, S. (2000). *Nothing like it in the world: The men who built the transcontinental railroad 1863–1869.* New York, NY: Touchstone.

Anderson, W. (1983). *The price of liberty: The public debt of the American Revolution* (Ist ed.). Charlottesville, VA: University Press of Virginia.

Andreas, P. (2013). *Smuggler nation: How illicit trade made America.* Oxford, US: Oxford University Press.

Bair, S. (2012). *Bull by the horns: Fighting to save main street from wall street and wall street from itself.* New York, NY: Free Press.

Baker, D. (2009). *Plunder and blunder: The rise and fall of the bubble economy.* Sausalito, CA: PoliPoint Press, LLC.

Bamber, B., & Andrew, S. (2008). *Bear trap: The fall of Bear Stearns and the panic of 2008.* New York, NY: Brick Tower Press.

Bandler, J., & Nicholas, V. (2009). How Bernie did it. *Fortune 159*(10), 51–71.

Barofsky, N. (2012). *Bailout: An insider account of how Washington abandoned main street while rescuing wall street.* New York, NY: Free Press.

Barr, A., & Irving, G. (1987). McKesson & Robbins. *Journal of Accountancy.* 159–161.

Barton, D. (2003). *Business and its environment* (VIth ed.). Upper Saddle River, NJ: Prentice Hall.

Bentson, G., & Hartgraves, A. (2002). Enron: What happened and what we can learn from it. *Journal of Accounting and Public Policy 21*(2), 105–127.

Berenson, A. (2003). *The number: How the drive for quarterly earnings corrupted wall street and corporate American.* New York, NY: Random House.

Bernanke, B. (2004). *Money, gold, and the great depression.* Retrieved 2004, from www.federalreserve.gov

Bernanke, B. (2009). *Financial innovation and consumer protection.* Retrieved April 17, 2009, from www.federalreserve.gov

Bernanke, B. (2009). *The financial crisis and community banking.* Retrieved March 20, 2009, from www.federalreserve.gov

Bernstein, P. (2005). *Wedding of the waters: The Erie Canal and the making of a great nation.* New York, NY: W.W. Norton & Company.

Blinder, A. (2013). *After the music stopped: The financial crisis, the responses, and the work ahead.* New York, NY: The Penguin Group.

Bodenhorn, H. (2006). Bank chartering and political corruption in antebellum New York: Free banking as reform.In Glaeser, Edward and Claudia G. (Eds.), *Corruption and reform: Lessons from America's economic history.* Washington, US: National Bureau of Economic Research.

Bookstaber, R. (2007). *A demon of our own design: Markets, hedge funds, and the perils of financial innovation.* Hoboken, NJ: John Wiley & Sons.

Brands, H. W. (2010). *American colossus: The triumph of capitalism, 1865–1900.* New York, NY: Doubleday.

Bremmer, I., & Nouriel, R. (2009). *How the fed can avoid the next bubble.* Retrieved October 5, 2009, from The Wall Street Journal: www.online .wsj.com

Brill, S. (2010, July 12). On sale: Your government. Why lobbying is Washington's best bargain. *Time*, pp. 28–35.

Brunner, R., & Sean, C. (2007). *The panic of 1907: Lessons learned from the market's perfect storm.* Hoboken, NJ: John Wiley & Sons.

Brunnermeier, M., & Martin, O. (2012). *Bubbles, financial crises, and systemic risk, Working Paper 18398.* Cambridge, MA: National Bureau of Economic Research.

Cassell, C., Gary, G., Linda, M., & Thomas, O. (2012). The effect of corporate governance on auditor-client realignments. *Auditing: A Journal of Practice & Theory 31*(2), 1–22.

Cassidy, J. (2009). *How markets fail: The logic of economic calamities* (Ist ed.). New York, NY: Farrar, Straus and Giroux.

Cassidy, J. (2009). *Rational irrationality: The real reason that capitalism is so crash-prone.* Retrieved October 5, 2009, from The New Yorker: www.newyorker.com

Chernow, R. (1990). *The house of Morgan: An American banking dynasty and the rise of modern finance.* New York, NY: Atlantic Monthly Press.

Chernow, R. (2004). *Alexander Hamilton.* New York, NY: The Penguin Press.

Chernow, R. (2009). *Where is our Ferdinand Pecora?* Retrieved January 6, 2009, from The New York Times: www.nytimes.com

Christensen, B., Glover, S., Omer, T., & Shelley, M. (2013). *Field evidence on auditors' and investors' views on audit quality.* College Station, TX: Unpublished Manuscript, Texas A&M University.

CNBC. (2010). *Top ten investor traps.* Retrieved April 9, 2010, from CNBC: www.cnbc.com/id/35988341/.

Cohan, W. (2009). *House of cards: A tale of hubris and wretched excess on wall street.* New York, NY: Doubleday.

Colbert, D. (2001). *Eyewitness to wall street: Four hundred years of dreamers, schemers, busts and booms.* New York, NY: Broadway Books.

Collier, C., & James, C. (1986). *Decision in Philadelphia: The constitutional convention of 1787.* New York, NY: Ballantine Books.

Colvin, G. (2010, March). Alan Greenspan fights back: From main street to wall street to the beltway, the former fed chief has been the "Designated goat" for the country's financial woes. Now the maestro takes on his critics. *Fortune,* 82–89.

Committee of Sponsoring Organizations of the Treadway Commission. (1987). *Report of the national commission on fraudulent financial reporting.* New York, NY: COSO.

COSO. (1999). *Fraudulent financial reporting: 1987–1997 – An analysis of US public companies.* New York, NY: COSO.

Cramer, J. (2002). *Confessions of a street addict.* New York, NY: Simon & Schuster.

Department of the Treasury. (2009). *Financial regulatory reform: A new foundation: rebuilding financial supervision and regulation.* Washington, WC: Treasury Dept.

Dos Passos, J. (1972). Robert Morris and the art magick. In, *Great stories of American businessmen, from American heritage.* New York, NY: American Heritage Publishing Co.

Editors of Fortune magazine. (2009). *Fortune: Scandal! amazing tales of scandals that shocked the world and shaped modern business.* New York, NY: Time Inc. Home Entertainment.

Eichenwald, K. (2005). *Conspiracy of fools.* New York, NY: Broadway Books.

Ellis, C. (2008). *The partnership: The making of Goldman Sachs.* New York, NY: The Penguin Press.

Ellis, J. (2008). *American creation: Triumphs and tragedies at the founding of the republic.* New York, NY: Alfred A. Knopf.

Fabozzi, F. (2005). *The handbook of mortgage-backed securities.* New York, NY: McGraw-Hill Professional.

Federal Reserve Bank of St. Louis. (Undated.) *The financial crisis: A timeline of events and policy actions.* Retrieved from timeline.stlouisfed.org

Feldman, N. (2010). *Scorpions: The battles and triumphs of FDR's great Supreme Court justices.* New York, NY: Twelve (Hachette Book Group).

Ferguson, E. J. (1971). *The American Revolution: A general history, 1763–1790.* Homewood, OK: The Dorsey Press.

Ferguson, N. (2008). *The ascent of money: A financial history of the world.* New York, NY: The Penguin Press.

Ferguson, N. (2011). *Civilization: The west and the rest.* New York, NY: The Penguin Group.

Financial Crimes Enforcement Network. (2006). *Mortgage loan fraud: an industry assessment based upon suspicious activity report analysis.* From www.fincen.gov.

Frank, B. (2010). *H.R. 4173: Dodd-Frank wall street reform and consumer protection act.* Retrieved December 2, 2010, from www.govtrack.us/congress

Frank, T. (2012). *Pity the billionaire: The hard-times swindle and the unlikely comeback of the right.* New York, NY: Picador.

Freeland, C. (2012). *Plutocrats: The rise of the new global super-rich and the fall of everyone else;* New York, NY: The Penguin Press.

Friedel, F. (1990). *Franklin D. Roosevelt: A rendezvous with destiny.* Boston, MA: Little, Brown and Company.

Friedman, M. (1970). *The social responsibility of business is to increase its profits–New York Times magazine.* Retrieved September 13, 1970, from www.colorado. edu/studentgroups/libertarians/issues/friedman-soc-resp-business.html

Friedman, T. (2000). *The lexus and the olive tree.* New York, NY: Anchor Books.

Fox, J. (2009, September). The bailout's biggest flaw. *Time,* pp. 44–45.

Fox, J. (2009). *The myth of the rational market: A history of risk, reward, and delusion on wall street.* New York, NY: Harper Business.

Furth, B., Lessing , L. & H. Vind (2009). McKesson and Robbins: Its Fall and Rise. *Fortune,* May 1940, reprinted in *Scandal! Amazing Tales of Scandals That Shocked the World and Shaped Modern Business,* Time Inc.

Galbraith, K. (1988). *The great crash 1929.* Boston, MA: Houghton Mifflin.

Gasparino, C. (2005). *Blood on the street: The sensational inside story of how wall street analysts duped a generation of investors.* New York, NY: Free Press.

Gasparino, C. (2009). *The sellout: Three decades of wall street greed and government mismanagement destroyed the global financial system.* New York, NY: Harper Business.

Gasparino, C. (2009). *Three decades of subsidized risk: There's a reason Dick Fuld didn't believe Lehman would be allowed to fail.* Retrieved November 6, 2009, from The Wall Street Journal: online.wsj.com

Geisst, C. (2000). *Monopolies in America: Empire builders & their enemies from Jay Gould to Bill Gates.* Oxford, US: Oxford University Press.

Geisst, C. (2009). *Collateral damaged: The marketing of consumer debt to America.* New York, NY: Bloomberg Press.

Gentzkow, M., Glaeser, E., & Goldin, C. (2006). The rise of the fourth estate: How newspapers became informative and why it mattered. In G. Edward, and C. Goldin (Eds.), *Corruption and reform: Lessons from America's economic history.* Washington, DC: National Bureau of Economic Research.

Gibson, C. (2001). *Financial reporting & analysis* (VIII ed.). Cincinnati, OH: South-Western College Publishing.

Giroux, G. (1996). *Dollars & scholars, scribes and bribes: The story of accounting.* Houston, TX: Dame Publications.

Giroux, G. (1998). Annual reports of the Minehill and Schuylkill Haven Railroad Company: 1844-1864. *The Accounting Historians Notebook,* 9–10, 30–33.

Giroux, G. (2003). *Financial analysis: A user approach.* New York, NY: John Wiley & Sons.

Giroux, G. (2004). *Detecting earnings management.* New York, NY: John Wiley & Sons.

Giroux, G. (2006). *Earnings magic and the unbalance sheet: The search for financial reality.* New York, NY: John Wiley & Sons.

Giroux, G. (2008). What went wrong? Accounting fraud and lessons from recent scandals. *Social Research: An International Quarterly of the Social Sciences* 75(4), Winter, 1205–1238.

Giroux, G. (2013). *Business scandals, corruption, and reform: An encyclopedia.* Santa Barbara, CA: Greenwood.

Giroux, G., & Cory, C. (2011). Changing audit Risk Characteristics in the Public Client Market. *Research in Accounting Regulation* 23(2), 177–183.

General Accounting Office. (2002). *Financial statement restatements: Trends, market impacts, regulatory responses, and remaining challenges (GAO-03-138).* Washington, DC: GAO.

Gilman, H., & Burke, D. (2010, May). Wall street 2010: A fortune roundtable moderated by CNBC's Becky Quick. *Fortune,* 190–200.

Gibby, D. (2012). *Why has America stopped inventing.* New York, NY: Morgan James.

Gladwell, M. (2005). *Blink: The power of thinking without thinking.* New York, NY: Little, Brown & Company.

Gladwell, M. (2008). *Outliers: The story of success.* New York, NY: Little, Brown & Company.

Gladwell, M. (2009). *What the dog saw and other adventures.* New York, NY: Little, Brown and Company.

Glaeser, E., & Claudia, G. (2006). *Corruption and reform: Lessons from America's economic history.* Washington, DC: National Bureau of Economic Research.

Gleeson-White, J. (2011). *Double entry: How the merchants of Venice created modern finance.* New York, NY: W.W. Norton & Company.

Goldberg, R. (2009). *The battle for wall street: Behind the lines in the struggle that pushed an industry into turmoil.* Hoboken, NJ: John Wiley & Sons.

Golden, T., Skalak, S., & Clayton, M. (2006). *A guide to forensic accounting investigation.* Hoboken, NJ: John Wiley & Sons.

Goodwin, J. (2003). *Greenback: The almighty dollar and the invention of America.* New York, NY: Henry Holt and Company.

Gordon, J. (1989). *The public be damned.* Retrieved September/October 1989, from American Heritage: www.americanheritage.com.

Gordon, J. (1999). *The great game: The emergence of wall street as a world power, 1653–2000.* New York, NY: Scribner.

Gordon, J. (2004). *An empire of wealth: The epic history of American Economic Power.* New York, N.Y.: Harper Collins Publishers.

Government Accountability Office. (2002). *Financial statement restatements: Trends, market impacts, regulatory responses, and remaining challenges.* Washington, D.C.: GAO.

Government Accountability Office. (2007). *Information on recent default and foreclosure trends for home mortgages and associated economic and market developments, GAO-08-78R.* Retrieved October 16, 2007, fromwww.gao.gov

Greenspan, A. (2004) *Speech at America's community bankers annual convention, Washington, D.C.* Retrieved October 19, 2004, from http://www.federalreserve.gov/BoardDocs/Speeches/2004/20041019/default.htm

Greenspan, A. (2007). *The age of turbulence, adventures in a new world.* New York, NY: The Penguin Press.

Healy, P., & Wahlen, J. (1999). A review of the Earnings management literature and its implications for standard setting. *Accounting Horizons,* 365–383.

Henninger, D. (2010). *Bring back the robber barons.* Retrieved March 4, 2010, from The Wall Street Journal: finance.yahoo.com

Henry, D. (2002, October 14). Mergers: Why most big deals don't pay off. *Business Week,* 60–70.

Henry, D., & Goldstein, M. (2007, December). The bear flu: How it spread. *Business Week.*

Hermanson, R., Strawser, J., and Strawser, R. (1993). *Auditing Theory and Practice.* Homewood, Il.: Irwin.

Huffington, A. (2003). *Pigs at the trough: How corporate greed and political corruption are undermining America.* New York, NY: Crown Publishers.

(1929). *Investment Trusts.* Retrieved February 4, 1929, from Time: www.time.com

Irwin, N. (2013). *The alchemists: Three central bankers and a world on fire.* New York, NY: The Penguin Press.

Johnson, S. (2005). *The quiet coup.* Retrieved May 2005, from The Atlantic:www.theatlantic.com

Johnson, S., & Kwak, J. (2010). *13 Bankers: The wall street takeover and the next financial meltdown.* New York, NY: Pantheon Books.

Johnston, D. (2012). *The fine print: How big companies use "Plain English" to rob you blind.* New York, NY: Portfolio/Penguin.

Jones, J. J. (1991). Earnings management during import relief investigations. *Journal of Accounting Research 29*(2), 193–228.

Josephson, M. (1962). *The robber barons.* New York, NY: Harcourt, Inc.

Keynes, J. (1933). An open letter to President Roosevelt. Retrieved December 31, 1933, New York Times: newdeal.feri.org

Kindleberger, C., & Aliber, R. (2005). *Manias, panics, and crashes: A history of financial crises* (Vth ed.). Hoboken, NJ: John Wiley & Sons..

King, T. (2006). *More than a numbers game: A brief history of accounting.* Hoboken, NJ: John Wiley & Sons.

Krugman, P. (2009). *The return of depression economics and the crisis of 2008.* New York, NY: W.W. Norton.

Law, M., & Libecap, G. (2006). The determinants of progressive era reform: The pure food and drugs act of 1906. In E. Glaeser and C. Goldin (Eds), *Corruption and reform: Lessons from America's economic history.* Washington, DC: National Bureau of Economic Research.

Levitt, A., & Dwyer, P. (2002). *Take on the street: What wall street and corporate America don't want you to know.* New York, NY: Pantheon Books.

Levitt, S., & Dubner, S. (2009). *SuperFreakonomics.* New York, NY: William Morrow.

Lewis, M. (1989). *Liar's poker: Rising through the wreckage on wall street.* New York, NY: Penguin Books.

Lewis, M. (2009). *Panic: The story of modern financial insanity.* New York, NY: W.W. Norton & Co.

Lewis, M. (2010). *The big short: Inside the doomsday machine.* New York, NY: W.W. Norton.

Livesay, H. (1978). *Samuel Gompers and organized labor in America.* Boston, MA: Little, Brown and Company.

Livesay, H. (2000). *Andrew Carnegie and the rise of big business.* New York, NY: Longman.

Lowenstein, R. (2004). *Origins of the crash: The great bubble and its undoing.* New York, NY: Penguin Press.

Lowenstein, R. (2010). *The end of wall street.* New York, NY: The Penguin Press.

MacLeish, A. (2009). The Swedish Match King. *Fortune,* May-July 1933, reprinted in *Scandal! Amazing Tales of Scandals That Shocked the World and Shaped Modern Business,* New York: Time Inc.

Mahar, M. (2004). *Bull: A history of the boom and bust, 1982–200.* New York, NY: Harper Business.

McCartney, L. (2008). *The teapot dome scandal: How big oil bought the Harding white house and tried to steal the country.* New York, NY: Random House.

McCullough, D. (1981). *Mornings on horseback.* New York, NY: Simon & Schuster.

McDonald, D. (2009). *Last man standing: The ascent of Jamie Dimon and JP Morgan Chase.* New York, NY: Simon & Schuster.

McDonald, L., & Robinson, P. (2009). *A colossal failure of common sense: The inside story of the collapse of Lehman Brothers.* New York, NY: Crown Business.

McGee, S. (2010). *Chasing Goldman Sachs: How the masters of the universe melted wall street down and why they'll take us to the brink again.* New York, NY: Crown Business.

McLean, B. (2009). The fall of Fannie Mae. *Fortune,* January 24, 2005, in *Fortune: Scandal! Amazing Tales of Scandals That Shocked the World and Shaped Modern Business,* New York: Time Inc. Home Entertainment.

McLean, B., & Nocera, J. (2010). *All the devils are here: The hidden history of the financial crisis.* New York, NY: Portfolio/Penguin.

McNichols, M. F. (2000). Research design issues in earnings management studies. *Journal of Accounting and Public Policy 19*(4–5), 313–345.

Menes, R. (2006). Limiting the reach of the grabbing hand: Graft and growth in American cities, 1880-1930. In E. Glaeser and C. Goldin (Eds), *Corruption and reform: Lessons from America's economic history.* Washington, DC: National Bureau of Economic Research.

Mitchell, L. (2007). *The speculative economy: How finance triumphed over industry.* San Francisco, CA: Berrett-Koehler Publishers.

Morgenson, G., & Rosner, J. (2011). *Reckless endangerment: How outsized ambition, greed, and corruption led to economic Armageddon.* New York, NY: Times Books.

Morris, C. (2008). *The trillion dollar meltdown.* New York, NY: Public Affairs.

Morris, E. (1979). *The rise of Theodore Roosevelt.* New York, NY: Random House.

Morris, R. (2003). *Fraud of the century: Rutherford B. Hayes, Samuel Tilden, and the Stolen Election of 1876.* New York, NY: Simon & Schuster.

Mulford, C., & Comisky, E. (2002). *The financial numbers game: detecting creative accounting practices.* New York, NY: John Wiley & Sons.

Mund, V. (1965). *Government and business* (IVth ed.). New York, NY: Harper and Row.

Murphy, K. (2012). *Executive compensation: Where we are, and how we got there.* Retrieved August 12, 2012, from http://papers.ssrn.com/sol3/papers.cfm?abstract_id=2041679

Myers, J., Myers, L., & Omer, T. (2003). Exploring the term of the auditor-client relationship and the quality of earnings: A case for mandatory auditor rotation? *The Accounting Review 78*(3), 779–799.

Office of the Special Inspector General for the Troubled Asset Relief Program. (2009). *Quarterly report to congress* Retrieved July 21, 2009, from www.sigtarp.gov

Partnoy, F. (1997). *FIASCO: Blood in the water on wall street.* New York, NY: W.W. Norton & Company.

Partnoy, F. (2003). *Infectious greed: How deceit and risk corrupted the financial markets.* New York, NY: Henry Holt and Company.

Partnoy, F. (2009). A revisionist view of Enron and the sudden death of "May". In *Enron and other corporate fiascoes: The corporate scandal reader* (IInd ed.). New York, NY: Thomson Reuters/Foundation Press.

Partnoy, F. (2009). *Derivative dangers.* Retrieved March 25, 2009, from www.npr.com

Paton, W., & Littleton, A. (1940). *An introduction to corporate accounting standards.* New York, NY: American Accounting Standards.

Patterson, S. (2012). *Dark pools: High-speed traders, A.I. Bandits, and the threat to the global financial system.* New York, NY: Crown Business.

Patterson, S. (2010). How the "Flash Crash" echoed black Monday. *Wall Street Journal*, A–1.

Paterson, S. (2010). *The quants: How a new breed of math wizards conquered wall street and nearly destroyed it.* New York, NY: Crown Business.

Paulson, H. (2010). *On the brink: Insider the race to stop the collapse of the global financial system.* New York, NY: Business Plus.

Penman, S. (2001). *Financial statement analysis & security valuations.* Boston, MA: McGraw-Hill Irwin.

Perkins, E. (1994). *American public finance and financial services, 1700–1815.* Columbus, OH: Ohio State University Press.

Phillips, K. (2008). *Bad money: Reckless finance, failed politics, and the global crisis of American capitalism.* New York, NY: Penguin Group.

Previts, G., & Merino, B. (1998). *A history of accountancy in the United States.* Columbus, OH: Ohio State University Press.

Pujo Committee Report. (1913). *Money trust investigation: Investigation of financial and monetary conditions in the United States under house resolutions Nos. 429 and 504.* Retrieved February 26, 1913, from fraser.stlouisfed.org

Rayner, R. (2008). *The associates: Four capitalists who created California.* New York, NY: W.W. Norton.

Reinhart, C., & Rogoff, K. (2009). *This time is different: Eight centuries of financial folly.* Princeton, NJ: Princeton University Press.

Renehan, E. (2005). *Dark genius of wall street: The misunderstood life of Jay Gould, king of the robber barons.* New York, NY: Basic Books.

Report of the committee on banking and currency. (1934). *Stock Exchange Practices.* Retrieved June 6, 1934, from fraser.stlouisfed.org/docs/publications/sensep/19340606_sensep.rpt.pdf.

Revsine, L., Collins, D., & Johnson, W. (2002). *Financial reporting & analysis* (IInd ed.). Upper Saddle River, NJ: Prentice Hall.

Ritholtz, B. (2008). *How SEC regulatory exemptions helped lead to collapse.* Retrieved September 18, 2008, from bigpicture.typepad.com.

Robertson, R. (1973). *History of the American economy* (IIInd ed.). New York, NY: Harcourt Brace Jovanovich.

Robinson, E. (2010). *Disintegration: The splintering of black America.* New York, NY: Doubleday.

Rosenberg, D. (2012). Delaware's expanding duty of loyalty and illegal conduct: A step towards corporate social responsibility. *Santa Clara Law Review 3*(1), 81–103.

Roubini, N., & Mihm, S. (2010). *Crisis economics: A crash course in the future of finance.* New York, NY: The Penguin Press.

Sandel, M. (2009). *Justice: What's the right thing to do?* New York, NY: Farrar, Straus and Giroux.

Schilit, H. (2002). *Financial shenanigans: How to detect accounting gimmicks & fraud in financial reports* (IInd ed.). New York, NY: McGraw-Hill.

Schipper, K. (1989). Commentary: Earnings management. *Accounting Horizons 3*, 91–102.

Schultz, E. (2011). *Retirement heist: How companies plunder and profit from the nest eggs of American workers.* New York, NY: Portfolio/Penguin.

Schweizer, P. (2011). *Throw them all out: How politicians and their friends get rich off insider stock tips, land deals, and cronyism that would send the rest of us to prison.* New York, NY: Houghton Mifflin Harcourt.

Securities and Exchange Commission. (2005). *Report and recommendations pursuant to section 401(c) of the Sarbanes-Oxley Act of 2002 on arrangement with off-balance sheet implications, special purpose entities, and transparency of filings by issuers.* Washington, DC: SEC.

Shiller, R. (2005). *Irrational exuberance* (IInd ed.). Princeton, NJ: Princeton University Press.

Skidelsky, R. (2009). *Keynes: The return of the master—Why, sixty years after his death, john maynard keynes is the most important economic thinker for America.* New York, NY: Public Affairs.

Sloan, A. (2009, November 9). What's still wrong with wall street. *Time*, pp. 24–29.

Sloan, A. (2010, May). How to really fix wall street. *Fortune*, 54–60.

Smith, R. (2009). The great electrical conspiracy. In *Fortune scandal!: Amazing tales of scandals that shocked the world and shaped modern business.* New York, NY: Time Inc.

Sobel, R. (1968). *Panic on wall street: A history of America's financial disasters.* Washington, D.C.: Beard Books.

Sobel, R. (2000). *The pursuit of wealth: The incredible story of money throughout the ages.* New York, NY: McGraw-Hill.

Sorkin, A. (2009). *Too big to fail: The inside story of how wall street and Washington fought to save the financial system from crisis—and themselves.* New York, NY: Viking.

Sorkin, A. (2010). *Preparing for the next big one.* Retrieved June 29, 2010, from The New York Times: www.nyt.com

Standard & Poor's. (undated). *S&P/Case-Shiller home price indices.* Retrieved from us.spindices.com/index-family/real-estate/sp-case-shiller.

Stewart, J. (1992). *Den of thieves.* New York, NY: Simon & Schuster.

Stiglitz, J. (2003). *The roaring nineties: A history of the world's most prosperous decade.* New York, NY: W.W. Norton.

Stiles, T. J. (2009). *The first tycoon: The epic life of Cornelius Vanderbilt.* New York, NY: Vintage Books.

Stiglitz, J. (2010). *Freefall: America, free markets, and the sinking of the world economy.* New York, NY: W.W. Norton.

Strine, L. (2012). *Our continuing struggle with the idea that for-profit corporations seek profit.* Retrieved April 14, 2012, from Wake Forest Law Review: wakeforestlawreview.com

Surowiecki, J. (2004). *The wisdom of crowds.* New York, NY: Doubleday.

Swartz, M., & Watkins, S. (2003). *Power failure: The inside story of the collapse of Enron.* New York, NY: Doubleday.

Taibbi, M. (2009). *The great American bubble machine.* Retrieved July 14, 2009, from Rolling Stone: www.rollingstone.com

Taleb, N. (2007). *The black swan: The impact of the highly improbable.* New York, NY: Random House.

The Economist. (2009). *A hard climb.* Retrieved September 6, 2009, from *The Economist*: www.economist.com.

The Financial Crisis Inquiry Commission. (2011). *The financial crisis inquiry report.* Washington, D.C.: U.S. Government Printing Office.

Tice, F., & Tse, S. (2013). *Are directors held accountable for oversight failure? New evidence on reputational penalties in the Post-SOX Era.* College Station, TX: Unpublished Manuscript, Texas A&M University.

(1955). *Sachems & sinners: an informal history of Tammany Hall.* Retrieved August 22, 1955, from Time: www.time.com

Toffler, B. (2003). *Final accounting: Ambition, greed, and the fall of Arthur Andersen.* New York, NY: Broadway Books.

Treasury Department. (2008). *Blueprint for a modernized financial regulatory structure.* Retrieved March 2008, from www.treas.gov

Tully, S. (2013, July). *The rebirth of fannie and freddie. Fortune*, 91–95.

U.S. Census Bureau. *Statistical abstract of the United States (various years).* Retrieved from www.census.gov

Varchaver, Nicholas (2009). The Big Kozlowski. *Fortune*, November 18, 2002, reprinted in *Fortune: Scandal! Amazing Tales of Scandals That Shocked the World and Shaped Modern Business.* New York: Time Inc. Home Entertainment.

Wallis, J. (2006). The concept of systemic corruption in American history. In E. Glaeser and C. Goldin (Eds.), *Corruption and reform: Lessons from America's economic history,* Washington, DC: National Bureau of Economic Research.

Watts, R., & Zimmerman, J. (1986). *Positive accounting theory.* Englewood Cliffs, NJ: Prentice-Hall.

Wessel, D. (2009). *In fed we trust: Ben Bernanke's war on the great panic.* New York, NY: Crown Business.

Willoughby, J. (2000). *Burning up.* Retrieved June 20, 2000, from Baron's: http://adage.com/article/news/barron-s-offers-follow-burning/9658/

Zeff, S. (2003). How the U.S. accounting profession got where it is today, part I. *Accounting Horizons 17*(3), 189–205.

Zeff, S. (2003). How the U.S. accounting profession got where it is today, part II. *Accounting Horizons 17*(4), 267–286.

Zuckerman, G. (2009). *The greatest trade ever: The behind-the-scenes story of how John Paulson defied wall street and made financial history.* New York, NY: Crown Business.

Zuckoff, M. (2006). *Ponzi's scheme: The true story of a financial legend.* New York, NY: Random House Trade Paperbacks.

Index

H
Hague, F., 34
Hamilton, A., 29, 31, 145
Hamon, J., 47
Hancock, J., 156, *n*1
Harding, W.G., 147
Harrison, G., 54
HealthSouth fraud (2003), 118, 152
The Home Owners' Loan
    Corporation (1933), 124
Homestead Strike of 1892, 19
Hoover, H., 54
Hospitality Franchise Systems (HFS),
    87
hostile takeovers, 77–79
housing, and mortgages, 123–124
housing bubble bust, 127

I
Iksil, B., 154
illicit behavior, 10
Imclone Systems case, 111, 151
incentives
    to cheat, ix
    commissions, 9–10
income statement, 4
incorporation laws, xi
Insull, S., 7, 55, 58, 148
Insull Utility bankruptcy (1931), 148
Insull Utility Investments, 57–58
interest payments, 3
internal controls, auditing part,
    114–115
internal revenue scandal (IRS, 2013),
    154
Internal Revenue Service (IRS), 50, 56
International Match Company
    (IMCO), 56
International Telephone and
    Telegraph (ITT), 76
Interstate Commerce Commission,
    xi, 64
Interstate Commerce Commission
    Act (1887), 146
investment banking, 71
investment banks, problems and
    solutions, 129
Investment Trust, 58–59

Investor Overseas Services fraud
    (APB, 1959), 148
Investors Overseas Services (IOS),
    82–84

J
Jackson, A., 14
Jamestown Colony, 28
Japanese manufacturing system, 3
JDSU (JDS Fitel and Uniphase
    merger), 110
Jefferson, T., 31
Johnston, D., 12
Joint Energy Development
    Investments (JEDI), 104
joint stock company, 1
junk bonds, 15, 80–81

K
Kaufmann, D., 7
Kaufmann index, of legal corruption, 7
Keating, C., 82
Kennedy, J.F., 63
Kinder Morgan case, 158, *n*4
Kinder, R., 103, 158, *n*4
Knickerbocker Trust Company, 46
Kohlberg, Kravis, and Roberts (KKR),
    79, 81
Kozlowski, D., 107, 151
10-K report, 3–4
Kreuger and Toll (KT), 55
    collapse, 148
    financial failings of, 56–57
Kreuger Crash, 57
Krueger, I., 148
10-Ks, 114, 116

L
laissez faire state, 25
late trading, 120
Lay, K., 100
Leeson, N., 90
legal corruption, 7
Lehman Brothers failure (2008), 17,
    129–130, 139, 153
Leonard, J. W., 12
leveraged buyouts (LBOs), 77, 79–80
libertarianism, 19–20

OTHER TITLES IN OUR FINANCIAL ACCOUNTING AND AUDITING COLLECTION

Scott Showalter, NC State University and Jan Williams, University of Tennessee, Collection Editors

- *An Executive's Guide for Moving from US GAAP to IFRS* by Peter Walton
- *Effective Financial Management: The Cornerstone for Success* by Geoff Turner
- *Financial Reporting Standards: A Decision-Making Perspective for Non-Accountants* by David Doran
- *Revenue Recognition: Principles and Practices* by Frank J. Beil
- *Accounting for Derivatives and Hedging Activities* by Frank J. Beil

FORTHCOMING IN THIS COLLECTION

- *Accounting for Business Combinations 1/15/2014* by Frank J. Beil
- *Accounting for Capital Transactions: An Issuer's Perspective 5/15/2014* by Frank J. Beil
- *The Use of Fair Value Measurements in Accounting 7/15/2014* by Frank J. Beil

Announcing the Business Expert Press Digital Library

*Concise E-books Business Students Need
for Classroom and Research*

This book can also be purchased in an e-book collection by your library as
- a one-time purchase,
- that is owned forever,
- allows for simultaneous readers,
- has no restrictions on printing, and
- can be downloaded as PDFs from within the library community.

Our digital library collections are a great solution to beat the rising cost of textbooks. e-books can be loaded into their course management systems or onto student's e-book readers.

The **Business Expert Press** digital libraries are very affordable, with no obligation to buy in future years. For more information, please visit **www.businessexpertpress.com/librarians**. To set up a trial in the United States, please contact **Adam Chesler** at *adam.chesler@ businessexpertpress.com* for all other regions, contact **Nicole Lee** at *nicole.lee@igroupnet.com*.

CPSIA information can be obtained at www.ICGtesting.com
Printed in the USA
BVOW03s1323051114

373529BV00010B/12/P